Processes in Third Language Acquisition

Processes in Third Language Acquisition

Edited by Björn Hammarberg

Edinburgh University Press

© editorial matter and organisation Björn Hammarberg, 2009

Edinburgh University Press Ltd
22 George Square, Edinburgh

www.euppublishing.com

Typeset in Ehrhardt
by Servis Filmsetting Ltd, Stockport, Cheshire, and
printed and bound in Great Britain by
CPI Antony Rowe, Chippenham and Eastbourne

A CIP record for this book is available from the British Library

ISBN 978 0 7486 3511 5 (hardback)

Contents

Preface

This volume presents a series of studies of an adult multilingual speaker who acquires a new language through social interaction. Five of the chapters have been published individually as articles at diverse places and are now gathered here together with an introduction and an added sixth chapter. They all emanate from a project conducted at Stockholm University which, as it matured, was named *Processes in Third Language Acquisition*.

This project started in 1990 when the young British linguist Sarah Williams arrived in Sweden to take up a job at Stockholm University and was faced with the need to learn Swedish. She saw this at the same time as an opportunity to document her progress in a new language from the outset. To this end, she and the present writer started to audio-record conversations in Swedish between the two of us at regular intervals in order to compile a longitudinal language corpus. This was continued for two academic years. During this time, we refrained from performing any analyses on the material, just aiming to bring together a broad corpus of semi-spontaneous conversational speech for later study. Sarah thus came to perform the methodologically rather unusual, but manifestly fruitful role of first serving as a language learner and supplier of data, and later, when the data collection was finished and her competence in Swedish was stronger, acting as a researcher of her own previous language performance together with the present writer.

Although we did not want to engage in any premature analyses of specific findings, it became clear early on that we had to do with a characteristic case of L3 acquisition. Sarah had grown up in England and her first language was English. She had studied languages at university and through this and a six-year stay in Germany had achieved near-native proficiency in German. (Her language background and how we define the concept of L3 will be explained in detail in the following.) It turned out that Sarah's use of Swedish displayed a complex pattern of crosslinguistic interaction between Swedish and her prior languages, including a strong component of German influence on her Swedish. In addition, she turned out to be very active in trying to communicate and to acquire the language in the speech situations, which has yielded a rich body of data to study. Our research interest came to centre on the patterns of crosslinguistic influence during the process of speaking and on Sarah's acquisitional activities in this multilingual setting.

Very sadly, and to the detriment of the project, Sarah Williams died prematurely in December 1996 at the age of thirty-four. A couple of studies had been completed, and others were being prepared. We had discussed several findings and ideas between us. The later contributions in the series are attempts to follow up the project as it had evolved and to develop it further along these lines.

The chapters in this book form what is commonly called a case study. But to us who worked together with Sarah and got to know her as a person, she was of course not a 'case', but a much appreciated colleague and friend. People surrounding her at the time will remember her bright intellect and keen curiosity, her delightful humour, the vivid discussions, the passionate way in which she played jazz on the saxophone, and many memorable episodes. It is also significant contribution of hers to have made it possible to document and explore a few aspects of how she as a multilingual speaker tackled the task of acquiring a new language.

Björn Hammarberg

Acknowledgements

The first five chapters in this book originate from earlier papers which are mentioned below; the sixth chapter was written for this book. The authors and editor wish to thank the persons and publishing houses who have been helpful in producing the original papers and have permitted reproduction in the present volume.

Chapter 1, 'A study of third language acquisition', originally appeared in *Problem, Process, Product in Language Learning, Papers from the Stockholm–Åbo Conference, 21–22 October 1992*, ed. B. Hammarberg, Stockholm University, Department of Linguistics (1993), pp. 60–70.

Chapter 2, 'Language switches in L3 production: Implications for a polyglot speaking model', appeared in *Applied Linguistics* 19/3: 295–333 (1998), published by Oxford University Press. The study was essentially completed when the first author, Sarah Williams, died in 1996. Thanks are due to Theo Bongaerts, Kees de Bot and Nanda Poulisse as well as three anonymous reviewers for valuable comments on an earlier version of the 1998 paper.

Chapter 3, 'Re-setting the basis of articulation in the acquisition of new languages: A third-language case study', was published in *Introductory Readings in L3*, ed. B. Hufeisen and R. J. Fouser, Tübingen: Stauffenburg Verlag (2005), pp. 11–18. This was a revised and updated version of a paper titled 'Articulatory re-setting in the acquisition of new languages', written for the *Studies Presented to Claes-Christian Elert on the Occasion of his Seventieth Birthday*, issued as *Reports from the Department of Phonetics University of*

Umeå (PHONUM), 2, ed. E. Strangert, M. Heldner and P. Czigler (1993). The authors are grateful to Sarah Williams for reading the 1993 manuscript and making valuable comments. Thanks also to Edelgard Biedermann, Christine Frisch and Frank-Michael Kirsch for judging the tape-recorded German passage, and to Gessica De Angelis for calling our attention to some details in the paper that needed clarification.

Chapter 4, 'The learner's word acquisition attempts in conversation', appeared in *Perspectives on Foreign and Second Language Pedagogy: Essays Presented to Kirsten Haastrup on the Occasion of her Sixtieth Birthday*, ed. D. Albrechtsen, B. Henriksen, I. M. Mees and E. Poulsen, Odense: Odense University Press (1998), pp. 177–90. Thanks are due to the University Press of Southern Denmark for the permission to reproduce the paper.

Chapter 5, 'Activation of L1 and L2 during production in L3: A comparison of two case studies', is an English translation of the paper 'Activation de L1 et L2 lors de la production orale en L3: Étude comparative de deux cas', which appeared in *L'acquisition d'une langue 3*, ed. R. Rast and P. Trévisiol, a thematic issue of the journal *Acquisition et Interaction en Langue Étrangère (AILE)* 24, published by L'Association ENCRAGES, Paris (2006), pp. 45–74. Thanks are due to an anonymous reviewer of the French paper for constructive comments.

A preliminary version underlying Chapter 6, 'The factor "perceived crosslinguistic similarity" in third-language production: How does it work?' was presented at the Fifth International Conference on Third Language Acquisition and Multilingualism, 3–5 September 2007, in Stirling, Scotland. The author is grateful to Jean-Marc Dewaele and Håkan Ringbom for valuable comments on this occasion.

List of tables

Introduction

Björn Hammarberg

In the last few years, systematic research on third language acquisition has gained momentum and attracted increasing attention as a crucial part of the wider field of individual multilingualism.[1] The studies presented here zoom in on the acquisitional activities of the individual learner and the patterns of crosslinguistic influence which arise in the multilingual setting.

WHY A THIRD LANGUAGE PERSPECTIVE?

Non-native language acquisition has for the most part been studied in terms of *foreign* or *'second' language acquisition* (SLA). Even if it is understood that learners often know more languages, the possible influence of prior non-native languages on the process of acquisition has in the past been assumed by most SLA linguists to be insignificant, and hence usually disregarded. The learner's *first language* (L1) was the only background language to which attention was paid. In this tradition all cases of non-native language acquisition were analysed as *second language* (L2) acquisition, and no difference was made between a previously monolingual and a bi- or multilingual language learner. The concepts of L2 and SLA came to cover non-native languages generally.[2] The upcoming focus on *third language* (L3) acquisition means that researchers have begun to differentiate learners according to the complexity of their linguistic background.

There are a range of reasons for the interest in L3 acquisition. For the sake of the discussion we may distinguish practical, theoretical and empirical types of motives.

Practical motives. We know that many people face the need to acquire more than two languages, not least in the modern European society. This applies, for example, to bilingual members of indigenous minorities and immigrant groups who study a foreign language at school, and also monolinguals who take their second or further foreign language. Moving between countries causes many people to need to learn a new language. International contacts have increased enormously, which both necessitates and furthers a repertoire of languages for larger numbers of individuals. The increasing role for English as a *lingua franca* in Europe and throughout the world puts English in the role of a third language for large groups of previously bilingual speakers (Cenoz and Jessner 2000). But the third-language role of course applies to other languages as well. Many educational questions arise in connection with the learning of third languages, for example how to devise language instruction for minority and immigrant students, how to understand and analyse their learning problems, and how to design adequate teacher education for these purposes. Some cognitive questions have practical implications: does a bi- or multilingual background have a beneficial effect on the learning of further languages, and if so, in what ways? (For an overview of this issue, see Cenoz 2003a.) Will language learners be metalinguistically more aware if they have already acquired a second language, and what does this imply? (See Jessner 2006, for a detailed treatment.) The need to approach language teaching from a wider perspective than the traditional model of target language instruction for a homogeneous group of monolingual speakers has become gradually more apparent.

Theoretical motives. The fundamental theoretical aspect of the study of L3 competence, use and acquisition is the insight that *humans are potentially multilingual by nature* and that *multilingualism is the normal state of linguistic competence.*

It has been assumed that bi- or multilingualism is at least as frequent in the population of the world as pure monolingualism, probably even more frequent. Several authors make this claim in the literature on bilingualism even if it is, of course, difficult to document with any precision (see for example Grosjean 1982: vii;

Hakuta 1986: 4–6; Cook 1992: 578; de Bot 1992: 2; Tucker 1998: 4; Aronin and Singleton 2008: 2). Mackey (1967) gives some relevant support for such an assumption by discussing the reasons why individual bilingualism is bound to be a very common situation in the world. (With bilingualism he includes multilingualism.) He points to the multitude of small linguistic communities, the wide currency and usefulness of the national and international languages, and people's increasing mobility across language borders. It is also obvious that all humans possess the capacity to learn several languages. Persons with knowledge of four, five or more languages are, as we all know, by no means exceptional. Aronin and Singleton (2008) argue that multilingualism in the world today, in the present era of globalisation, has reached an unprecedented scale and significance in society, to the point that it can be characterised as a new world order, or a new linguistic disposition, as they prefer to call it.

Given that humans are potentially multilingual by nature, an adequate theory of language competence, use and acquisition should be able to account for multilingual cases, and preferably take these as the norm, treating pure bi- and monolingualism as special cases. The theory will have to take into account that the (linguistically mature) individual may normally have two or more languages to handle, and that (a) the speaker is able to choose according to intention which language to use, (b) the speaker's languages can regularly be kept apart, but also get mixed or influence each other, and furthermore (c) that the person's competence in the various languages will normally not be at equal levels. In view of this, the language acquisition process in multilinguals becomes a significant field of study, particularly the ways in which the individual's languages interact in such complex cases.

Empirical motives. If we are to study speakers' complex language competence and use, including how languages develop and attrite in the speaker's mind and interact in the performance process, we will obviously get a more complete picture if we adopt a multilingual rather than a bilingual perspective. We will simply be able to see more and pose more questions. For example, in studying how the speaker's languages interact in the speaking process and in interlanguage development, we may examine which languages take part in the process, to what extent and why, if the speaker's

L1 has a privileged role (as implicitly assumed in most studies of crosslinguistic influence in the past), if on the other hand, there is a particular reliance on prior L2 knowledge (an 'L2 status effect', a phenomenon we will deal with in Chapters 2, 5 and 6 below), and so forth. Also the cognitive abilities touched upon above, such as metalinguistic awareness, linguistic creativity, communicative and acquisitional strategies and so on, are bound to be more extensively researchable in a multilingual than in a bilingual setting.

A NOTE ON CONCEPTS AND TERMINOLOGY

The term *third language* (L3) is used variably in the literature. Since it is not self-evident what kind of concept the term can refer to, there is reason to reflect somewhat on terminology.

One common practice is to number the speaker's languages chronologically, according to the time of first encounter: L1, L2, L3, L4 and so on. This may be satisfactory for certain practical purposes in cases where a linear order of this kind can be established. Thus, for example, L3 may be the next language acquired by a person raised with two languages, or the second foreign language at school for a monolingually raised child. This chronological scale may seem parallel to the terms monolingual, bilingual, trilingual, quadrilingual and so forth, which represent the result of the acquisition of a certain number of languages. But the analogy is superficial. The problem is that it will often be neither meaningful nor even possible to order a multilingual's languages along a linear time scale. Multilingualism has a different kind of complexity. Here are some aspects of this which may defy linear ordering:

- Simultaneous acquisition: How can we order languages which are encountered at the same time and acquired in parallel?
- Scanty knowledge: By what criteria shall we count or exclude languages of which the person knows 'a little'?
- Intermittent or alternating acquisition: It is not uncommon for persons to become acquainted with a language gradually in different periods of life interspersed with the acquisition of other languages. It may be hard to establish an order of priority here.

- Type of knowledge: How should languages be judged of which the person essentially has a particular type of command, for example reading knowledge? Or the type of cultural, metalinguistic or non-communicative knowledge that may, for example, be the case with Latin?
- Bonus languages: Should we count languages which come 'into the bargain' because they are very close to a language the person knows? An example would be the Scandinavian case: if you know Swedish, you will fairly easily understand Norwegian and Danish and get used to occurring differences.

It will be clear from these points that the languages of multilinguals are very often not easily numbered on a linear time scale. Both purely chronological problems and uncertainty whether to count or exclude a language contribute to this difficulty. The linear numbering practice may be handy in specific given contexts, for example when dealing with foreign languages at school (provided possible other languages acquired outside school do not make facts more complicated). But even so, this terminology remains provisional and lacks generality.

A different approach is based on the conventional use of the notions of L1 and L2, where L1 refers to a language established up to a certain level in infancy, and L2 to any language encountered and acquired after infancy. The cut-off point when an L1 can be said to be 'established' will have to be set by a chosen criterion, for example an age criterion such as three years as proposed by McLaughlin (1984: 10). A person can have one or more L1s and one or more L2s. Here the distinction is based on different stages in the person's life, and not on a language-by-language chronology. The need to distinguish between the acquisition of an L2 in the narrow sense – the first beyond an L1 – and the acquisition of further languages motivates a separate term for the latter case. One practice is therefore to use the term L3 to cover any language from the third onwards. Some authors have used a somewhat more specified term to integrate the third and further languages, such as 'L≥3' (Fouser 2001) or 'third or additional language' (De Angelis 2007). The rationale for just distinguishing three different categories – L1, L2 and L3 – is the view that the acquisition of a third language is qualitatively different from the acquisition of a second due to the prior experience with a non-native language, but that the addition of further languages does not make any radical difference in this respect (cf. Hufeisen 1998: 171f).[3]

The terminology adopted in the present work dispenses entirely with the linear model. Instead it connects with the conventional use of the notions of L1 and L2 and takes notice of the qualitatively different conditions for language acquisition in the mono-, bi- and multilingual. A *multilingual* is then defined as a person with knowledge of three or more languages. A *first language (L1)* is any language acquired during infancy, and a *second language (L2)* any language encountered and acquired after infancy, as stated above. In dealing with the linguistic situation of a multilingual, the term *third language (L3)* will be used for a non-native language which is currently being used or acquired in a situation where the person already has knowledge of one or more L2s besides one or more L1s. An L3 is thus a special case of the wider category of L2, and not necessarily language number three in order of acquisition. It should be noted that the term L3 in this definition relates to a given situation of language use or acquisition by the learner(s) in question. The other L2s known by the L3 user at the time may then be termed 'prior L2s' or, when the context makes the meaning clear, just 'L2s'. The L1(s) and prior L2(s) will be subsumed as *background languages*. Terms like 'L4' will be unnecessary.

This terminology recognises that it is often justified to speak of even multilingual language learners as 'L2 learners' (in the sense of 'learners of a non-native language'), as the general practice has been so far. Clearly there are many topics within the established field of SLA where the complexity of the learner's language background is not a crucial aspect, and there is no need to oppose the conventional use of 'L2' in such cases. The notion of L3 is available when multilingualism is in focus.

One thing that is bound to complicate the use of terms in this area is the problem inherent in the term 'second language'. Looking back at the conventional use of this term, it appears to have been a somewhat unfortunate coinage from the very beginning. The literal meaning of the expression as 'language number two' tends to create confusion. The term seems to have been created in a social context where monolingualism was regarded as the normal case, one additional language was seen as something extra, and the case of possessing more languages was not even considered. As a consequence, the use of the term today in the sense of any language acquired after infancy has to be explained over and over again. The terms 'second language' and 'SLA' are certainly very firmly established today, but in the long run it might be worthwhile to opt for a more adequate terminology. One possibility to consider could be to replace the terms 'first', 'second' and 'third' language by *primary*, *secondary* and *tertiary* language, respectively. The abbreviations L1, L2 and L3 may well be kept with this interpretation. This could make it easier to avoid the confusion caused by the association of L2 with 'language number two' in a linear sequence of acquisition. Rather than being based on a language-by-language chronology, this terminology expresses a cognitive hierarchy between the languages for the user in the current situation. In this respect an L2 is secondary to L1, and an L3 is tertiary in relation to L1 and L2. These alternative terms have been used by some researchers and are thus not unknown in the field. In the present volume, however, we will remain with the established expressions 'first', 'second' and 'third' language and use them as defined above.

THE L3 USER-LEARNER

In this section, a few aspects of L3 acquisition which play a role in the subsequent studies will be pointed out.

For the individual speaker-listener, there is a cyclic interdependence between language use, acquisition and competence. Language use draws on language competence and feeds acquisition, which feeds competence, which feeds use, and so forth:

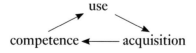

In principle, language *use* comprises *reception and comprehension* as well as *production* of utterances. In the present studies, however, we shall concentrate mainly on the production side, making use of a corpus of spoken conversations. Thus, while we shall be examining language performance in interpersonal exchange, we shall focus on the participants (in particular the L3 learner) as speakers, rather than as listeners. The distinction between reception and production processes is important to bear in mind, however, partly since decoding linguistic input occurring in a given context works under different conditions than encoding a self-generated message in linguistic form, and partly because the two types of process alternate and interact in the course of language acquisition. We shall return to this aspect later in this volume (Chapter 6).

A central issue concerns how the multilingual's performance relates to our understanding of *the speaking process*. Among recent models of speaking, Levelt's (1989, 1993, 1999) representation of the mature monolingual speaker has been particularly influential in L2 and L3 acquisition research. It spans the speaking process 'from intention to articulation' (the subtitle of Levelt's 1989 book) and also connects it to the process of speech comprehension. Adaptations of this monolingual model have been proposed for the bilingual speaker (de Bot 1992; Kormos 2006) and for the multilingual speaker (de Bot 2004, with particular reference to lexicon).

Language use involves the *activation* of parts of the person's language competence (words, sentence structures, set phrases, phonological properties and so on). Because language use causes spreading of activation to semantically and phonologically related items within and across languages, influence from co-active language elements may arise. Apart from the activation of specific elements of a language, a language as a whole will be more or less active in the speaking situation. Green (1986) distinguished schematically between a *selected* language (the one currently intended for use), an *active* language (one which is simultaneously present in the speaker's mind and can influence the performance process) and a *dormant* language (which is known to the speaker, but exerts no crosslinguistic influence). A central question is in what ways, and under what conditions a multilingual speaker's different background languages, and elements from them, are activated in the speaking process.

We assume that *L3 acquisition* is driven by language use. This is generally considered to proceed automatically for the most part, beyond the individual's conscious control. The basic mechanism will then be a usage-based procedure, in which language structure is gradually established and entrenched in the speaker's long-term memory through frequent use (that is comprehended reception and production) of utterances and elements of utterances (cf. Langacker 1988, 1999; Kemmer and Barlow 1999; Bybee and Hopper 2001; Ellis 2002; Bybee 1998 with reference to lexicon). However, besides assuming this automatic process, we can observe how a learner purposely strives to acquire elements of language by various means, motivated by communicative need or by mere curiosity. One method for this which we will study in the following is the attempt by the L3 learner in interpersonal interaction to elicit expressions from an interlocutor who masters the target language. This may take many forms. The study of the strategies applied here and of the linguistic outcomes provides insight into some processes of L3 acquisition (see Chapters 4 and 6).

The multilingual speaker-listener's linguistic competence is a *multicompetence*, a term used by Cook (1991, 1992) to denote 'the compound state of a mind with two grammars' (1991: 112); it should be equally applicable to more than two grammars. Psycholinguistic research in recent years supports what de Bot (2004) terms *non-selective access* to words, that is multilinguals access words from their different languages in parallel, rather than searching one language at a time (see de Bot 2004 for a review of research). This means that 'words from more than one language can compete for activation both in production and perception' (de Bot 2004: 23). The different languages are considered to constitute *subsets* within the same cognitive system (Paradis 1981). Words (lemmas) in the lexicon are assumed to be tagged with labels to identify which language they belong to (Green 1986; Poulisse and Bongaerts 1994).

At the same time, it is possible to speak of hierarchical relations between the multilingual's languages. On the one hand, there is a hierarchy of acquisition which becomes relevant in the performance situation. There are the source languages, already stored in the speaker's mind: the L1(s), the prior L2(s) and the accumulated L3 interlanguage, which are primary, secondary and tertiary in the sense suggested above. And there is the L3 as input language in reception and as target language in production and acquisition. On the other hand, the language user experiences a hierarchy of language activation, the selected/active/dormant hierarchy as proposed by Green. In the present project, we found that *one* of the learner's background languages can assume a favoured role in influencing her production in L3.

This brings up another distinction, which we found important in dealing with the learner's use of background languages, that between an *instrumental* and a *supplier* role. A multilingual speaker, especially in a multilingual mode (Grosjean 2001), may switch selected language for various practical ('instrumental') purposes. This should be distinguished from the crosslinguistic influence that a background language can exert on the selected language in the speaking situation. Only in the latter case does a background language have the role of supplier, that is, supplying material for formulations in the L3. Various interacting factors will determine which language will function in the role of instrument and supplier, respectively. We will deal with this in detail in the following (Chapters 2 and 5).

THE PROJECT *PROCESSES IN THIRD LANGUAGE ACQUISITION*

The work reported here is an exploratory case study of an L3 learner of Swedish, based on a longitudinal corpus of Swedish conversations between the learner Sarah Williams (SW) and the native speaker Björn Hammarberg (BH). In one of the chapters below (Chapter 5), we will also study another learner, using comparative data extracted from another corpus.

SW started acquiring Swedish at the age of twenty-eight when she arrived in Stockholm to work as a university teacher. Her L1 was British English. Her prior L2s were German (near-native competence), French (advanced, but not used for a long time), and Italian (elementary). Although a linguist by training, SW did not engage in theoretical, formal study of Swedish, but acquired the language in her everyday life and in her job.

SW and BH met for recording sessions on thirty-five occasions during twenty-one months (two academic years), starting fourteen days after SW's arrival in Sweden. This means that SW's Swedish speech production has been documented over time from the beginner stage to a well developed and fluent, although not yet error-free stage. In the first month, the sessions took place about once a week, and then gradually somewhat less often; a detailed time schedule can be seen in Tables 2.5–2.7 in Chapter 2. The recorded talks comprise SW's narrations of wordless picture stories in interaction with BH as well as conversations on various topics connected to her everyday life and personal experiences. Some of the picture stories were re-used on a later occasion so as to allow longitudinal comparisons on the same task.

The recordings were transcribed and stored on computer in a modified orthographic form, applying a set of transcription conventions and special symbols which are explained in Appendix 1 at the end of the book. The transcripts were made by a phonetically trained assistant (the same person throughout the corpus) and checked jointly by SW and BH while replaying the tapes. The transcribed corpus comprises circa 55,000 word tokens in total: 37,000 from SW and 18,000 from BH.

In addition to the conversations proper, introspective observations by SW were also collected during the sessions. This material has not been analysed in full and cannot be fully accounted for in this volume. But a brief presentation of this part and some findings will be given in Chapter 1.

During the two years when the text corpus was being compiled, no linguistic analysis was performed on the material, nor did we attempt to identify specific hypotheses or phenomena to study. This was decided in order not to unnecessarily affect the spontaneity of the speaking situations and influence language acquisition. After the period of corpus compilation, SW had reached a level of competence in Swedish which made her fully capable of researching her earlier Swedish performance.

THE PRESENT VOLUME

The following chapters contain a collection of papers in which findings from the L3 project have been reported over the years. They have been slightly edited so as to fit better together in a volume. The last chapter has been written for this book. Some repetitions of background facts should enable the reader to study the chapters separately.

Chapter 1 is an early presentation of the project. One reason for its inclusion here is that it contains a section on the collection of introspective data (of the type 'immediate retrospection'), a part of the wider project not reported on elsewhere. We discuss the reliability and value of this method, and provide some observations that connect to the rest of the project.

Chapter 2 presents a detailed study of the learner's use of *language switches* (code-switching into English and German) during the conversations in Swedish. The learner made abundant use of such switches, particularly in the early stages of L3 development. The switches were found to differ in nature according to their pragmatic purposes, and so did the involvement of the background languages. Switches to L1 English occurred predominantly in various types of pragmatically purposeful switches, wheras seemingly automatic, non-intentional switches usually involved L2 German. These latter switches are interpreted to be part of the learner's formulation attempts in L3. Other observations, too, indicate that the L2 knowledge of German tended to be active during utterance formulation in Swedish. There was even an amount of observed German influence on inserted English utterances during these conversations, something which underscores the strong co-activation of a prior L2 in this speech situation. The findings are discussed in relation to recent models of the speaking process. In this chapter, a functional role division for the speaker's languages is proposed, distinguishing between an *instrumental role* (as evidenced in pragmatic language switches, used for metalinguistic and metacommunicative purposes) and a *supplier role* (supplying linguistic material for formulations in the target language). In this multilingual study it becomes clear that these different roles need not involve the same background language. Further, the interaction of factors causing a particular language to predominate in the supplier role is discussed, and it is suggested that the language's *L2 status* (the property of being an L2 for the learner) is one important such factor, besides factors of proficiency, recent use and similarity to L3. The longitudinal development is also treated in this study, and it is shown that as time goes on, the activation of background languages weakens, and the instrumental and supplier roles are more and more taken over by the L3 itself.

Chapter 3 is a short phonetic study of the learner's performance.

Phonetic studies with specific focus on an L3 context are so far quite rare. The chapter deals with the phenomenon of *articulatory settings* (*Artikulationsbasis*), that is, the language-specific positions and gestures of the voice and articulatory organs in speech, and the speaker's ability to acquire new such settings for a new language. These subphonemic but transsegmental properties are important for the impression whether the pronunciation sounds right for the language in question, and in case it does not, the settings can often be traced back to a specific background language. This longitudinal study demonstrates the workings of articulatory settings in SW's speech at the initial stage of L3 acquisition, where settings from the prior L2 German are seen to play a significant role, and at a later stage which is more characterised by influence from L1.

The fourth chapter examines the learner's interactive behaviour in the speech situations, particularly regarding her attempts to obtain words in L3. SW was very active in seeking linguistic help from her interlocutor during the conversations, and also in testing hypotheses by offering tentative L3 words. The study focuses on metalinguistic passages in the dialogue where the learner acts strategically to elicit vocabulary from the native L3 speaker, and to retain words that she obtains in this way. Such passages are very frequent, and they are shown to be systematically structured and to display characteristic, regular patterns. A range of more or less explicit means of elicitation are applied. Two main strategies are *language switches* and *hypothetical word constructions*. Self-repairs, step-by-step construction of forms, explicit and implicit questions and other elicitative signals are also used regularly. The ways in which the various means function and interact are demonstrated and discussed. The question, to what extent the learner actually retains the acquired items over time, is also addressed; this is an issue which has proved difficult to explore and hence is seldom addressed in related research. When the involvement of the background languages is examined, the characteristic role division proposed in Chapter 2 is confirmed here: L1 English dominates in the instrumental role and L2 German in the supplier role with this learner. Finally, the point is made that the means that the learner applies in word elicitation are not specific to learners; what we observe is just maximal use of interactive and linguistic means which are natural even to mother-tongue speakers.

Case studies need to be validated by other investigations that deal with the same issues. A first systematic attempt to compare the case of SW with that of another learner is made in the fifth chapter. It has a focus on how the background languages are activated in the L3 speaking process. This chapter also expands the discussion in earlier chapters of the speaking process in multilinguals and of the various conditioning factors which interact to assign an instrumental or a supplier role to a language. The new learner, called EE, had German as L1, English as an early L2 and Swedish as his current L3. He thus had the same main background languages as SW, but in a different order of acquisition. Another difference is that EE became bilingual with German and English during childhood, whereas SW acquired her L2 German at a later age. EE's language production was gathered from another longitudinal corpus which had been built up in a similar way as in the case of SW. The results reveal that the two learners show partly different patterns of activating their respective L1 and L2 when communicating in L3. The outcome of the comparison again confirms the relevance of distinguishing an instrumental and a supplier role for background languages. One particular finding is that the 'L2 status factor' seems to be less significant in EE's case. This is interpreted as being related to the difference in language acquisition history between the two learners, EE being an early bilingual and SW a late L2 learner.

The sixth and last chapter draws attention to the relations between the languages involved, taking a close look at the factor of *crosslinguistic similarity,* also known as the *typology* factor. Among the various factors that may promote influence from L1 or prior L2 knowledge on the acquisition of an L3, this is the one most often referred to in the literature. The relatively greater similarity between a particular L1 or L2 and the current L3 may lead to a dominant influence from that language. However, the similarity as perceived by the learner (the *psychotypology*) is not simply equal to the 'objective' similarity between languages that can be established through language descriptions. It is an empirical issue to determine how a learner perceives and exploits crosslinguistic similarity. If two background languages are at very uneven typological distance from the L3, the discrepancy between objective and perceived similarity may not matter much; the close language will reasonably exert more overall influence on L3 performance than the distant one, other factors being equal. But with languages at more even distance, the question is more open. English and German are both relatively similar to Swedish, structurally and culturally, although each of them has its areas of greater similarity or dissimilarity. This provides an opportunity to study in more detail how a learner perceives and evaluates crosslinguistic similarities. The chapter takes a new look at SW's attempts to construct hypothetical words in situations where she searches for formulations in L3. Unlike Chapter 4, where such instances were primarily examined from the perspective of the learner's interactive strategies, we this time study them from the point of view of their linguistic content and the speaking process. A characteristic pattern emerges, where the learner extends factual lexical similarities between Swedish and German, being less guided by existing similarities with English. The results also put a focus on the process of constructing words creatively while speaking, a significant aspect of lexical processing which has received remarkably little attention in research on the speaking process.

In sum, these different studies of L3 production in the individual will, I hope, shed light upon a number of aspects of L3 processing and provide some useful points of departure for future research on the multilingual language learner.

NOTES

1. The recent vivid interest in multilingualism and third language studies is reflected in a booming literature in the field and in efforts to organise scientific exchange particularly in this area. Thus, a series of biannual *International Conferences on Trilingualism and Third Language Acquisition* was started in 1999, leading to the formation of the *International Association of Multilingualism* in 2003 and the establishment of the *International Journal of Multilingualism* in 2004. Among publications in the field, several important anthologies have appeared, for example Cenoz, Hufeisen and Jessner (2001, on crosslinguistic influence, and 2003, on the multilingual lexicon), and Cenoz and Jessner (2000, on third language use and acquisition in present-day Europe, focusing on the role of English). A series of monographs

and anthologies, *Tertiärsprachen. Drei- und Mehrsprachigkeit/ Tertiary Languages and Multilingualism* has been issued since 1998, edited by B. Hufeisen and B. Lindemann and published by Stauffenburg Verlag in Tübingen.

2. This applies also to most studies in the subfield of *foreign language acquisition*. In the following, I will subsume *foreign language acquisition* and *second language acquisition in the narrow sense* under the common label *second language acquisition (SLA)*.

3. To what extent the knowledge of more langugages will change the conditions for further language acquisition is really an empirical issue; to my knowledge there is as yet no systematic research comparing language acquisition in bi-, tri- quadri- etc. -linguals, which could support or rule out the practice of treating the acquisition of third and further languages on a par. I think such research should be welcomed.

CHAPTER 1

A study of third language acquisition

Björn Hammarberg and Sarah Williams

Quite often, adult language learners are already familiar with one or more second languages at the point at which they start learning a new one. This type of situation is probably becoming even more frequent in the present-day society, due to several factors: an increase in travelling and working abroad, greater focus on languages in education, greater exposure to other languages through the media, and so on. Prior L2 knowledge is often mentioned as a source of influence on the acquisition of a new language. Despite this, there have as yet been very few comprehensive studies carried out in order to investigate the influence of previously learned second languages on the new language being learned (cf. the bibliography by Henriksson and Ringbom 1985, and the survey of previous research in Ringbom 1987: 112ff). This situation may be due to an assumption that the influence of prior L2 knowledge is generally weak or insignificant, or the difficulty in finding suitable situations in practice where the interaction between prior L1 and L2 knowledge and the developing new language can be studied.

In the following, we will distinguish between the *first language (L1)*, prior *second languages (L2s)*, and the language that the learner is currently acquiring, which we will label the *third language (L3)*. We will present an outline of a longitudinal case study of one learner's acquisition of Swedish as a third language, and give some examples to illustrate a few, as yet very preliminary findings.

1.1 L3 ACQUISITION

One reason for exploring L3 acquisition is that it may enhance our understanding of the acquisition processes, and processes of crosslinguistic influence in particular. The L3 situation provides an opportunity to study how a complex pattern of prior linguistic knowledge is utilised by the learner. Among the few existing substantial studies of L3 acquisition, there are two which involve Swedish as L2 in L3 acquisition. The first looks at Finnish students' German studies at Stockholm University and comprises part of the project on pedagogy in teaching German at university level, 'Tyskans universitetspedagogik' (TUP) (Biedermann and Stedje 1975; Stedje 1977). The second constitutes part of the project carried out at Åbo Akademi in which results are compared from Finnish-speaking and Swedish-speaking students of English (Ringbom 1985, 1987: 112–29, 146–62). Here, the constellations L1=Finnish, L2=Swedish, L3=English are compared with L1=Swedish, L2=Finnish, L3=English. Both of these projects are based on cross-sectional data taken from language tests.

The relative roles of L1 and L2 in influencing the acquisition of L3 appear to depend on a complex set of interacting factors. Below is a brief mention of some such determinants, based on findings reported in Stedje (1977) and Ringbom (1987).

1. *The degree of similarity between the languages concerned.* L2 is seen to exert stronger influence on the acquisition of L3 if it is closer to L3 than if it is more distant. Also, if L2 is more similar to L3 than is L1, the relative role of L2 tends to be stronger.
2. *Level of competence in L2.* The greater and more current the knowledge of L2, the greater its influence on the acquisition of L3.
3. *Natural setting for L2, and automatised skills in L2.* In addition to the amount of L2 knowledge, it seems that L2 influence on L3 is furthered if L2 has been acquired in a natural environment, rather than a foreign language learning environment. The automatised use of L2 is identified as a furthering factor.
4. *Oral versus written production.* As suggested by Stedje (1977: 154) and Ringbom (1987: 128), limited control in speech

situations causes crosslanguage influence to occur more often in speech than in writing.

5. *Type of language phenomenon.* 'Generally the cross-linguistic influence between non-native languages in a European context has been shown to occur primarily in lexis' (Ringbom 1987: 114). In both the Åbo and the Stockholm studies, various types of lexical/semantic problems are discussed. Broadly stated, for the Finnish-speaking learners in both projects, problems of 'word choice' tend to show influence from L1, whilst various problems concerning 'word form' tend to show influence from L2. Grammatical influence from L2 on L3 is found to be more limited, whereas such influence from L1 is fairly common. Phonological influence is reported to come predominantly from L1.

1.2 THE PRESENT STUDY

One of the authors, Sarah Williams (SW), has served as the subject in producing the data for our project. She is English and lived in Germany for six years before coming to Sweden in August 1990, when she began to learn Swedish in an informal context, that is in everyday life in a Swedish environment, without formal language teaching in Swedish. Her L1 is English, her main L2 is German (although she can also speak French and has learnt a little Italian) and her L3 is Swedish. This project traces the first two years of SW's development in Swedish.

SW is a clear example of a third language learner, as we have defined this concept here, and we have taken her encounter with Swedish as a given opportunity to study the nature of L3 acquisition. In view of the determinant factors mentioned above, the chances of L3 being influenced by both L1 and L2 are relatively great in our project. The three languages, English, German and Swedish, are all closely related to each other and, to a certain extent, are structurally similar. SW's German shows a high level of competence, fluency and automatisation, which was maintained during the period of our study through visits to Germany. We have concentrated on oral production. Our material, consisting mainly of free coherent speech, comprises all levels of language structure.

Since August 1990, we made recordings of SW's Swedish, which, during the first three months, took place roughly every week, and then roughly once every three weeks. Each recording comprised a natural conversation between SW and Björn Hammarberg (BH), who is a native speaker of Swedish, and the narration of a picture story, in the form of either a monologue or a dialogue. (In the early sessions we also included some other activities, such as reading; see below.) Each picture story was narrated again at a later point in time so that specific comparisons could be made when the data were analysed. This corpus, which covers a period of about two years, forms the basis for a longitudinal performance analysis.

In addition to this, introspective data were also collected during each recording session. These data took two forms, firstly SW's own general observations about her developing Swedish, recorded orally in the form of 'diary observations' and secondly, specific (textbound) comments pertaining to the material (conversation and picture story) that had just been recorded. Here, two tape recorders were used. The original material (conversation, picture story) was recorded on the first tape recorder. This was then played back, during which time both SW and BH could stop the machine to comment on any aspects of the language being heard. The whole of this activity, both the playing back and the comments made, was recorded on a second tape recorder. This introspective material will also be analysed and used as a complement to the corpus of L3 utterances.

1.3 INTROSPECTION

The use of introspective data in interlanguage analysis has to be handled with some care, the problem being how to take advantage of the 'inside information' from the learner without being seriously trapped by a subjective bias. On the other hand, introspective methods have often been employed in linguistic analysis, and recent concern with such methods in cognitive psychology (cf. Ericsson and Simon 1984) has also influenced second language research (see especially the contributions in Færch and Kasper 1987a). A typology of introspective methods in second language research, which is also a useful methodological guide, is given by Færch and Kasper (1987b).

Poulisse, Bongaerts and Kellerman (1987) discuss the issue of the reliability of retrospective data (which pertains especially to SW's textbound retrospective comments in our case). They specify the following requirements, based on Ericsson and Simon (1984):

1. the data should be collected immediately after task performance, when memory is still fresh;
2. the subjects should be provided with contextual information to activate their memories;
3. all the information asked for must be directly retrievable, i.e. it must have been heeded during task performance, so that the subjects are not induced to generate responses based on inferencing and generalisations;
4. for the same reason the information asked for should relate to specific problems, or a specific situation;
5. no leading questions should be asked, to minimise the effects of 'researcher bias';
6. the subjects should not be informed that they will be asked for retrospective comments until after task performance, so as not to affect their performance on the task.
   (Poulisse et al. 1987: 217)

Our project fulfils requirements 1–5 but not requirement 6. Requirement 6 obviously refers to single test situations. In a longitudinal study in which retrospection takes place regularly, the informant's knowledge that retrospection will occur is technically unavoidable. The question then arises as to whether introspection is too risky in this case. The risk obviously has to be acknowledged, but it should be measured against the potentially valuable information that can be gained from longitudinal data, and the possibilities of obtaining supporting evidence on specific points. We believe there are good reasons for not overemphasising this risk factor or allowing it to hinder the use of retrospection. Firstly, the commentaries take place in English; talking in Swedish and commenting on re-played passages in English becomes a routine with two separate activities. Both BH and SW have the strong impression that SW actually forgets about the introspective aspects during the conversation/narrative in Swedish and concentrates on what she is attempting to communicate. Secondly, during the entire period when data were being gathered, we avoided any deeper discussion of the linguistic phenomena with each other or analysis of either the performance data or the introspective data, as this could have influenced subsequent observations. Thirdly, the analysis of the introspective data will function as a complement to the analysis of the performance data and will be interpreted in relation to the latter, which may give us an idea of the relevance and weight of the introspective part in each case. An important methodological point here is that the introspective statements – like the L3 utterances – can be located in time and context.

Even if the conclusions we can draw from the combined consideration of L3 utterances and introspective comments are hypothetical for the time being and would need to be confirmed by further investigation, the introspective part may have a value because it may lead us to discover things which would not have been discovered on the basis of the L3 utterances alone.

1.4 SOME PRELIMINARY FINDINGS

While we intend to study several areas of language production and the processes involved, we shall present some preliminary findings here which relate especially to phonological influence of L1 and L2 on L3 at early stages.

We shall first present a few examples of observed data from the conversations and picture stories, then take into account SW's recorded introspective comments on these points which she made a few minutes afterwards, and finally consider the combined objective and subjective data.

1.5 OBSERVATION 1: PRONUNCIATION

During SW's first week in Sweden, a recording was made of her narration of a picture story, *Hunden* 'The dog'. As SW's knowledge of Swedish at this point was very minimal, this was prepared for in the same session by BH first doing the exercise himself, so that SW had had some input. A narration of the same picture story was recorded one year later. (The transcripts of the two recorded narrrations are given in Appendix 2 at the end of the book. For a key to transcription conventions, see Appendix 1.)

What is striking on comparing SW's pronunciation in these two recordings is that they give the impression of two markedly different 'foreign accents': predominantly German in the early one, and predominantly English in the later one. The difference is so salient that native Swedes, who listened to the two recordings without being informed in advance, thought that there were two subjects with different L1s, German in the first and English in the second recording. Specific sound segments, intonation contours and the voice quality were all reported to differ.

During the first recording session, SW also read two simple passages aloud from a Swedish language text book. This was arranged as two different types of task. The first passage was first read by a Swedish speaker to SW in small segments (about 3–6 words), each of which she then repeated immediately after having heard them. No such help was given with the second passage; SW simply read it out on her own.

Here, too, native Swedish listeners reported noticing a clear difference between the two readings. When SW read by repeating segments, however, her attempts to approximate the Swedish pronunciation did not sound especially German, but rather showed traces of English. However, when she read on her own, her pronunciation appeared markedly German.

A more detailed analysis and discussion of these two picture narrations and the two reading tasks will be given in Chapter 3.

1.6 OBSERVATION 2: LEXICON

During conversation and narration, SW often attempts to invent or construct lexical forms on her own. The interaction of various linguistic sources for these word creations is one of the areas we are planning to study. Particularly in the early period, SW sometimes makes use of lexical items which are unmistakably French in origin. Words such as *restaurant, fauteuil*, which actually do exist in more or less the same form in Swedish, *restaurang, fåtölj*, occur with a somewhat adapted pronunciation. An example in the first picture story is the verb *sjettar* 'throws'. Even considering only the recorded utterance, there is no doubt that the source is the French *jeter* 'throw', in which the initial voiced fricative has become a voiceless fricative and the stress and the stem vowel have been changed, thus yielding interlanguage-Swedish *sjettar* [ˈʃɛtar] as a present tense form (see Appendix 2, Passage 1).

1.7 OBSERVATION 3: MORPHOLOGY

An early phenomenon in SW's Swedish interlanguage is the use of *i* to represent definite article plural. This happens on several occasions, whereby the noun may occur with or without the Swedish definite plural suffix *-na*:

		Target form:	
i grannarna	*'the neighbours-the'*	grannarna	[0;0.29]
i personer	*'the persons'*	personerna	[0;0.29]

At the point at which this phenomenon emerges, it appears to be quite strong; even when confronted with the correct Swedish version, SW still uses *i* as plural definite article. Consider the following extract from a conversation in the second week in which SW is attempting to elicit the Swedish word form from BH. Both the pronunciation and the word ending reveal that SW is starting with the German *Studenten* 'students' as a model.

SW:	[ʃt-] [ʃ]tudenten. i [ʃ]tudenten?
BH:	mhm. studenterna.
SW:	i studenterna. [0;0.22]

Obviously, SW was focusing her attention on checking the noun form and was not then aware of any problem with *i*.

1.8 OBSERVATION 4: MORPHOLOGY

SW varies her infinitive forms in the early recordings. The predominant variants are standard Swedish forms (mostly ending in *-a*) and non-target forms ending in *-ar* or *-er* (variants often observed with other English speakers as well). But occasionally she uses interlanguage forms ending in *-are*, as in the following examples:

> ja tycker inte om skriv- skriv*are* mycke   [0;0.22]
> '*I don't like write- write much*'
>
> ja kan spel*are* min instrumenterna   [0;0.29]
> '*I can play my instruments*'

1.9 SW'S INTROSPECTIVE COMMENTS

A comment repeatedly made by SW is that she did not want to sound English in her first attempts to approximate the Swedish pronunciation, but would rather prefer to approach the sound of Swedish from the basis of another foreign language such as German.

In the retrospective interview after *Hunden* in the first week, SW attested that she had formed the verb *sjettar* from French *jeter*. But her comment on this also indicates that this choice of a French source was quite deliberate and related to phonological problems. In particular, she was searching for a word that might be viable as a Swedish word, and rejecting words which in her opinion would be phonologically too alien to Swedish. We quote a passage from the interview:

SW: I was going to say something German but that just didn't seem right, because I didn't have any recollection of you saying something like *werfen* and so I looked around for some other foreign-sounding word, and the only other language I can speak is French, so I came up with *jeter*. And then I thought 'I'll try a Swedish version of that'. I didn't want to use my English as a back-up, because something like *throw – throwa* – that wouldn't be – *throware*, or whatever the Swedish people would say – So I was looking round for possibilities of using foreign words that I know in a Swedish setting, and perhaps making them Swedish . . .

BH: And you were somehow reluctant to use English words, because you feel that they wouldn't fit?

SW: Yes, because it would just sound ridiculous . . .

SW: . . . I would never have thought of using *throw*. Perhaps because of the nature of the word *throw*, because it's got a *t h* and Swedish just doesn't happen like that. Whereas *jeter* – those words, those sounds might possibly be it in Swedish.

As for the article form *i* and the infinitive form with *-are*, SW did not observe them at the time, and BH avoided focusing attention on them. But later, when SW's attention was called to these forms, she explained them as coming from Italian.

1.10 DISCUSSION

First, it seems quite clear that L2 phonological influence on L3 acquisition *does* occur. Judging from the differences in pronunciation between the two narrations of *Hunden* (as well as informal observations of the early tapes yet to be carefully analysed), this phonological influence on L3 is prominent in the initial stage of L3 acquisition, and then gradually becomes weaker. We suspect that a reason why phonological L2 influence on L3 has hardly ever been mentioned in earlier studies (Ringbom 1987: 114) is that not enough attention has been paid to the initial phase of the learner's encounter with L3.

From early on, SW developed conceptions about what would be phonologically possible in Swedish, and these phonological intuitions were gradually refined as she gained more experience with Swedish. We suggest that this feeling for L3 phonology very quickly creates a *phonological filter* which guides the selection of both L2 and L1 elements which are potential candidates for incorporation into L3. SW's interpretation of the verb creation *sjettar* exemplifies this. This would also apply to the Italian-based morphological elements *i* and *-are*. SW's knowledge of Italian is mainly theoretical, but even this type of knowledge appears to function as a source of L2 influence on L3. The preposed definite article *i* has support morphologically from SW's prior languages: both English, German, French and Italian use preposed definite articles; Swedish is the first of SW's languages which requires a suffixed article. The Italian-inspired infinitive form ending in *-are* occurs with an adaptation to the Swedish stress pattern, for example ['speːlarə] instea' of *[spe'laːre].

The different pronunciation styles that SW displayed in the two read-aloud tasks suggests that the learner's tendency to make use of L2 in coping with L3 is in part task-related. This certainly is an aspect which remains to be explored further, but at least we can see that a performance situation in which fresh L3 input and interaction with a native L3 speaker is given, such as the read-after-me task, produces a different result than a situation where the L3 model is not present, such as the read-on-your-own task. In the former case, the learner naturally concentrates on interpreting the perceived input, whereas in the second case she is more dependent on previously established linguistic skills. This general conclusion may seem rather trivial, but the interesting point is the division of labour between L1 and L2 in the process. In the imitative reading task, the secondary language (German) apparently exerts little influence, but the phonetic categories in the primary language (English) cannot be entirely suppressed. In the read-on-your-own task, however, using German phonetic models seems to be SW's main strategy for coping with the unfamiliar L3, so that L2 influence suppresses L1 influence.

The use of L2 phonology in L3, then, seems more consciously controllable than L1 phonology and, in SW's case, is even used in an attempt to block L1 influence. This dominance pattern changes with time. Through increased input and usage of L3 and consequent refining and strengthening of the phonological filter, the insufficiency of using L2 as a phonological strategy is noticed by the learner, and this strategy is gradually dropped; more attention is now paid to the direct production of L3, without going through the agency of L2. The disappearance of this more or less conscious 'layer' of L2 removes the means of blocking L1 and results in an increase in unconscious phonological influence from L1, which would explain SW's gradual shift from a German to an English accent.

CHAPTER 2

Language switches in L3 production: Implications for a polyglot speaking model

Sarah Williams and Björn Hammarberg

2.1 INTRODUCTION

In the majority of studies of crosslinguistic influence in L2 acquisition, usually only the L1 is taken into account. In the case of a bilingual or polyglot, this may well be an oversimplification of the situation. A previously learned language (referred to here as an L2) may also have an influence on a learner's production in a new target language (referred to here as L3). The aim of the following is to explore similarities and differences in the occurrence of L1 English and L2 German in what we refer to as *non-adapted language switches* using a case study of the first two years of L3 production in an adult learner of L3 whose background languages are L1 English and L2 German, and to propose a developmental model of L3 production.

The influence of previously learned languages on a learner's production in the target language may show itself not only in the form of crosslinguistic influence on the learner's interlanguage (IL) but also in the non-target-language-adapted (non-TL-adapted) occurrence of non-L3 languages during target language production. Intentional language switching is referred to in the bilingualism literature in terms of code-switching, borrowing or language mixing. In the L2 literature such language switching is referred to largely in terms of communication strategies (Bialystok 1983; Færch and Kasper 1983) used by the learner to overcome problems arising from a limited lexicon. More recently, attention has also been drawn to non-intentional language switching (Poulisse and

Bongaerts 1994), although this has also been documented elsewhere earlier (for example, Vildomec 1963). Non-intentional blending of languages has also been explored by the Kassel group in terms of competing plans (see, for example, Dechert 1984, 1989). Research on non-adapted language switches in L2 acquisition shows that these can be due to various factors and thus have various functions, namely:

1. sociopsychologically motivated
2. proficiency-related (communication strategy, lack of TL knowledge; thematic continuity)
3. metalinguistic comments (communication strategy, thematic discontinuity)

As regards sociopsychological factors, given that L2 learners are acquiring not only the language but also skills in how to use the language, it is likely that they are at the same time developing code-switching strategies. In the literature on bilingualism, these are generally regarded as being intentional and governed by sociopsychological factors pertaining to the content of the message and the interaction situation. Code-switching may involve varying stretches of discourse from single words up to complete turns (Færch and Kasper 1983). This decision itself often contains information about speaker attitude and communicative situation. If an L1 item is adjusted to IL phonology and/or morphology, however, this no longer constitutes code-switching, but is referred to as *interlingual transfer* (ibid.: 47).

There is also the case of proficiency-related language switches, which occur particularly in L2 beginners and intermediate learners, as opposed to more advanced L2 speakers, with the function bridging the communication gap in those cases where the learner's knowledge of the L2 is not sufficient. Tarone et al. (1983) place them within a subgroup of communication strategies which they refer to as *avoidance strategies*. Avoidance strategies are defined as a 'means of getting around target language rules or forms which are not yet an established part of the learner's competence' (ibid.: 10).

As regards metalinguistic comment, in addition to the direct use of language switching in terms of incorporating an L1 element into the L2 target utterance, language switching may also be involved in metalinguistic communication, where the thematic continuity is broken in the sense that the communication situation itself is commented on. Færch and Kasper (1983) point out that conversations between learners and native speakers often contain a fair amount of metalinguistic communication and that problems in interaction can be solved by the learner's signalling the problem to his interlocutor in an attempt to get the problem solved on a cooperative basis. This kind of appeal has been referred to as 'self-initiated other-repairs' (Schegloff, Jefferson and Sacks 1977).

In addition to these three kinds of non-adapted switches, a fourth has been identified, referred to as 'non-intentional language switches' (Poulisse and Bongaerts 1994), 'performance switches' (Giesbers 1989, from Poulisse and Bongaerts 1994), 'slips of the tongue', 'accidental L1 substitutions' (Poulisse 1997), and 'automatic code-switching' (Vogel 1992) (cf. also Vildomec 1963; Stedje 1977; Ringbom 1985).

Poulisse and Bongaerts (1994), in a study of non-intentional language switches, operationalise the distinction in terms of hesitation phenomena and intonation. In this study, they analysed data from three groups of Dutch learners of English at three different proficiency levels: fifteen second-year university students of English (age nineteen to twenty-two), fifteen grade 11 pupils (age fifteen to sixteen) and fifteen grade 9 pupils (age thirteen to fourteen). The corpus consisted of circa thirty-five hours of speech (circa 140,000 words) and comprised data from a story retelling task, conversations with a native speaker of English, and two other tasks which required the speakers to refer to pictures of concrete objects and abstract shapes. It was found that the number of non-intentional language switches from the L1 were higher in the youngest group of pupils (who had had the least exposure to the L2) and lowest in the group of university students, who had had the most exposure. In addition, they found that, except for the group containing the subjects with the longest exposure to L2, function words were much more often involved in non-intentional non-adapted language switches than were content words,[1] which exceeded the ratio of function:content words in their corpus.

Of 749 cases of the non-intentional language switches, 316 related to function words and 302 related to editing terms which Poulisse and Bongaerts defined as being used by the speaker to comment on an error he had made or an inappropriate word he had used, and/or to warn the listener that what followed should be interpreted as a repair of what preceded (i.e. metalinguistic communication). The remaining 131 of the total 749 related to content words. This supports data from Giesbers (1989, from Poulisse and Bongaerts) showing that such switches tend to involve function words, and also from Pfaff (1979), who found that L1 switches in an L2 sentence tend to consist of function words, sentence adverbials, tags and interjections. Further findings from Poulisse and Bongaerts's data were that more content words were repaired than function words (53.4 per cent versus 30.7 per cent respectively), and content words tended to be repaired before completion more so than function words (68.6 per cent versus 15.5 per cent, respectively). TL-adapted language switches, on the other hand, in which the switched element is phonologically or morphologically adapted to the L2, involved very few function words, and appeared to be proficiency-related.

In short, there seem to be different kinds of language switches in L2 production which in turn may indicate that the L1 is being put to different uses. If this is so, what happens in the case of L3 acquisition, where the learner has not only the L1 but also one or several L2s which might be used? Is it only L1 that occurs in language switching, or does the L2 occur here too? If so, is L2 influence similar to L1 influence in terms of function and frequency?

2.2 BILINGUAL LANGUAGE PROCESSING MODELS

In this section, we will present de Bot's (1992) model of bilingual speech production, together with Poulisse and Bongaerts' (1994) critique and amendments to it, and we will discuss certain points which we regard as relevant for a developmental account of L3 production. (See Poulisse 1997 for a review of these and other bilingual processing models.)

De Bot's model is based on Levelt's (1989) 'Speaking' model, which is a model of speech in a monolingual situation. Levelt's model consists of four main components: a knowledge component, containing knowledge of the world and the interactional situation; a conceptualiser, in which preverbal messages are planned;

a formulator, which converts the preverbal message into a speech plan by selecting the right words or lexical units and applying grammatical and phonological rules; and an articulator, which converts the speech plan into actual speech. De Bot's aim is to apply the model to language processing in bilinguals but to change as little as possible of the original model, since this is well founded on empirical evidence.

De Bot contends that a bilingual version of Levelt's model should be able to account for several things: firstly, the fact that two language systems can be used separately or mixed; secondly, the existence of crosslinguistic influence; thirdly, the effects of different levels of proficiency; and lastly, the ability to cope with a potentially unlimited number of languages. A central question formulated by de Bot is which part of the system in Levelt's model is involved in choosing the language to be used in an utterance, and what information this choice is based on. He accepts that there is awareness of cultural differences in interaction at the level of the knowledge component, and that the latter may thus contain a 'discourse model', i.e. a list of limiting conditions for the speech which is to be generated. Since there are differences in concepts between languages, preverbal messages for the same speech intention for two languages may be different. Dismissing the idea that the preverbal message should contain all the possible relevant information for all possible languages for reasons of economy, de Bot assumes instead that it is in the first phase of processing in the conceptualiser, the macroplanning, that 'the language to be used is selected on the basis of information from the discourse model, and that accordingly language-specific encoding takes place in microplanning' (de Bot 1992: 8), i.e. the second phase of the conceptualiser's processing.

Here, de Bot incorporates Green's (1986) suggestion that the different languages in a polyglot can have three levels of activation: *selected* (controls the speech output), *active* (plays a role in ongoing processing, runs parallel to the selected language, but is not articulated) or *dormant* (not active during ongoing processing), and stresses an important aspect of Green's proposal, namely that

the active language does everything the selected language also does: it selects lexical items, forms sentences, generates surface structures and eventually even makes a phonetic plan. The only difference is that the phonetic plan of the active language is not fed into the articulator. (de Bot 1992: 13)

De Bot points out that the notion of parallel production is supported by findings from unilingual research into ambiguous words and speech errors. In summary, then, de Bot's bilingual model is such that the knowledge component sends information affecting language choice to the conceptualiser, which then selects one of the two languages. Both languages are then formulated in parallel but only the selected language is finally articulated.

Poulisse and Bongaerts' (1994) criticism of de Bot's model is twofold. Firstly, it is not clear how two alternative speech plans can be formulated in parallel if the information in the preverbal message raises the activation level of one of the languages only, and secondly, it is uneconomical to have speech plans being formulated in parallel, since in theory there need not be any limit to the number of alternative plans that are being produced. Following de Groot (1992), they suggest instead that lexical items belonging to different languages are related to common conceptual nodes, so that translation equivalents and semantically related words share all or a number of meaning elements, both within and between languages. They suggest further that the information concerning language choice is added to the preverbal message in the form of a language component which plays a role in the activation of individual lexical items:

> Thus, besides conceptual information activating particular lemmas, there will be an additional language component which spreads activation to the lemmas of that particular language. This implies that language is one of the features used for selection purposes, and hence that lemmas are tagged with a label which specifies to which language they belong . . . (Poulisse and Bongaerts 1994: 41).

In Poulisse and Bongaerts' model, then, the language tag provides the extra activation necessary to select a lemma from one language and prevent the other from being activated; in de Bot's model, lemmas from both languages are activated in parallel but only one of them is selected for articulation. Both models employ the same kind of mechanism, but involve suppression of competing elements at different levels. Poulisse and Bongaerts find their model more economical because the suppression of competing elements at an earlier stage in the model saves the extra processing load of double or multiple retrieval of lexemes and morphosyntactic information at lower levels in the model. Poulisse and Bongaerts support their model with reference to studies on word translation, semantic priming and slips of the tongue in L2 production and suggest that their model can account for the kind of non-intentional switches they found in their data.

Four factors are mentioned in order to account for findings that function words are more involved in unintentional language switches (or performance switches, as Giesbers refers to them) than content words, namely frequency, recency, attention and word length. Giesbers (1989, from Poulisse and Bongaerts) suggests that a contributory factor may be because L1 function words tend to be frequent. Poulisse and Bongaerts agree with Giesbers, and find this the most plausible explanation, pointing out that within a framework of spreading activation, high-frequency words and words that have been used very recently require less activation for lexical access than low-frequency words and non-recent words. However, this does not really explain why function words are more frequent in switches anyway; although function words in L1 will at least initially be more frequent than function words in L2, also content words in L1 will be more frequent than content words in L2. Also, as Wode et al. (1992) point out, closed-class items are acquired fairly quickly by L2 learners, these constituting circa 30 per cent or more of vocabulary items in the first month of L2 acquisition (Burmeister 1986, from Wode et al. 1992). Bearing this in mind, it is more likely that the explanation for the frequency of function words in performance lies elsewhere, and is related to a qualitative difference in these categories.

Poulisse and Bongaerts also discuss Giesbers' suggestion that function words may be more involved in language switches than content words because they carry less information, and beginning learners who may, because of limited attention, need to make a choice between items they are going to attend to may opt for the more meaningful content words, leaving the function words to look after themselves. Also, function words tend to be shorter than content words. This implies that they take less time to encode and articulate, which brings with it a lower probability that they will be intercepted before or during production. As a result, 'more slips will be made in the selection of function words and fewer slips involving function words will be discovered by the monitor and intercepted' (Poulisse and Bongaerts 1994: 47).

A problematic area in Poulisse and Bongaerts' discussion, however, is their claim to be able to explain Giesbers' performance switches as the erroneous access of an L1 item instead of an L2 item, and to suggest that such switches are very similar to lexical substitution errors involving semantically-related lexical items within one language. Giesbers posits that intentional switches take place in the conceptual module and non-intentional ones in the morphophonological module, as a result of errors in the specification of the intended lexeme. However, merely postulating that non-intentional switching into L1 during L2 speech is the result of erroneous access of an L1 item instead of an L2 is a description, not an explanation, and does not in itself necessitate their own particular model. Where do these errors come from? Poulisse and Bongaerts suggest that 'unintended switches to the L1 are, in fact, very similar to lexical substitution errors involving semantically-related lexical items like *low* and *high* and *fingers* and *toes*' (1994: 42). This, however, is problematic, as lexical substitution errors tend to involve mostly content words (Garman 1990) and unintended switches to the L1 involve mostly function words.

2.3 L3 ACQUISITION RESEARCH

At this point we would like to compare the nature of non-intentional language switches in L2 acquisition with the nature of non-intentional language switches in L3 acquisition. In accordance with the literature, we use the term L3 to refer to the language that the learner is currently acquiring (corresponding to the language under study), L1 to refer to the learner's native language, and L2 to refer to any other previously learned non-native languages.[2]

In recent surveys of second language acquisition research, the phenomenon of other known languages playing a role in the acquisition of a subsequent language is sometimes briefly mentioned, such as in Sharwood Smith's (1994: 198) definition of crosslinguistic influence as including 'the influence of any other tongue known to the learner of that target language' (cf. also Kellerman 1983: 113; Odlin 1989: 27; Ellis 1994: 11 and 339). There are a number of studies which are concerned with the question of whether bilinguals have an advantage over monolinguals in learning a subsequent language (see Klein 1995 for a short overview), but to date there still exist only relatively few studies of L3 acquisition in which the role of non-native languages is investigated. However, those which have been carried out show clear evidence of L2 influence, at various levels (for example Chandrasekhar 1965, 1978; Stedje 1977; Ringbom 1983, 1987; Hufeisen 1993; Vogel 1992; Williams and Hammarberg 1994; see also Chapters 1 and 3 of this volume).

The majority of the studies mentioned above, however, tend to focus on identifiable L2 influence in the learner's IL, with little mention of unintentional switches. The few studies of L3 acquisition which do mention unintentional language switches (Vildomec 1963; Ringbom 1982, 1983, 1987; Stedje 1977) indicate that, as in the case of L2 acquisition, it is predominantly function words that are involved. The interesting point here is that the majority of unintentional language switches seem to involve L2, and not L1.

Vildomec's (1963) work is based on observations from a large number of subjects, although there is no detailed empirical data. He observes that in early L3 production, functors such as prepositions, articles and conjunctions tend to come from the L2, not from the L1. He states that 'the tendency to transfer into an Le [*i.e. an L2 in our terminology*] short empty words from other Le's is especially strong. This transfer may occur even if the correct and incorrect words (and the material of the two languages as wholes) are rather dissimilar in sound' (1963: 170).

Ringbom's (1987) data are taken from around 11,000 English (L3) essays written by candidates from Finnish-language schools in the national matriculation examination in English, who had Swedish as an L2. In his corpus of lexical errors which he lists in an appendix, there are 187 instances of language switch (referred to by Ringbom as 'complete language shift') from Swedish L2, and only eight instances of language switching from Finnish L1. Of these 187 instances, 125 (67 per cent) can be identified as content words and sixty-two (33 per cent) as function words.[3] Ringbom found that the words which were the most frequent were the clause connectors *fast* (= 'although', thirteen instances), *men* (= 'but', ten instances) and *och* (= 'and', eight instances). He suggests that the existence of the English forms *fast* and *men*, although entirely different in meaning, may have influenced the writers, and also suggests lack of attention to form as a reason for why these items may be the most frequent automatic items: 'it may well be that such links between major elements get less close attention than the actual form into which the writer wants to put his main ideas. This would probably be even more so in spoken language' (Ringbom 1987: 122).[4] Ringbom notes that another frequently recurring type of language switch (twenty-two instances) involves words of foreign origin (for example *auktoritet, intressant*).

Stedje's (1977) data comprises fifty-five five-minute recordings of Finnish learners of L3 German who had learnt L2 Swedish in Finland, and had spent not more than four years in Sweden. Her data showed a large (in the paper unspecified) number of instances of language switch, which appear to be non-intentional, as often the spontaneously produced Swedish word would be immediately corrected by the speaker (for example *viele små, kleine Katzen*). Stedje notes that it is often Swedish function words which occur (for example *men, som, helt, för*). She found no such instances of language switches from Finnish L1. Stedje suggests that one possible factor in such occurrences may be that Swedish is more closely related to German than is Finnish, which belongs to a different language family. However, in this connection, it is worth noting that she also found those non-intentional language switches which came from Swedish to be far more frequent in the Finnish students with L2 Swedish than in the Swedish students with L1 Swedish. In the latter group of learners, it was predominantly L2 English function words which occurred in language switches (Stedje, personal communication).[5]

This is supported by anecdotal evidence from other L3 learners, including a case of Finnish L1, Swedish L2 and Estonian L3 (Päivi Juvonen, personal communication).[6] Estonian and Finnish are closely related to each other, whereas Swedish comes from a different language family. In the case of this subject, it would actually have been more successful to have used Finnish, both structurally and phonologically. Despite this, interference came primarily from L2 Swedish, and not L1 Finnish. This, although anecdotal, provides support for the notion that the L1/L2 status of a polyglot's other languages (i.e. whether the language is L1 or L2) may be at least as important as typological similarity in the occurrence of such switches.

If we compare these findings to findings concerning non-intentional language switches in L2 acquisition, we can see that in both L2 and L3 acquisition, non-intentional language switches consist mainly of function words. The interesting point as regards L3 acquisition is that these non-intentional switches appear to come predominantly from the L2, not from the L1. While it is possible that in the particular L3 cases documented, it is the similarity of the L2 to the L3 that is the major factor in automatic occurrences, Stedje's observation that in the learning of German, non-intentional Swedish switches occurred far more frequently in the case of L2 Swedish than in the case of L1 Swedish would indicate that the occurrence of L2 may have to do with not just language typology but also the L1/L2 status of the languages involved.

This means that we have to look more carefully at arguments based on considerations of frequency, as put forward by Poulisse and Bongaerts. Overall, it is likely that the L1 has been used at least as frequently as the L2, so if overall frequency were the determining factor, we would therefore expect L1 function words to occur in performance slips. If, on the other hand, typology were the main factor, then in Juvonen's case, Finnish rather than Swedish would have been activated, and, in Stedje's study, L1 Swedish would presumably have occurred as much as L2 Swedish in the acquisition of L3 German. However, from the evidence presented above, this is apparently not the case; it is predominantly L2 words which occur.

2.4 DIFFERING ROLES OF L1 AND L2 IN L3 ACQUISITION

We posit that L1 and L2 may play essentially different roles in L3 acquisition. In the case of L3 acquisition, the assignment of functional status of the various languages during online production simply in terms of *selected, active* and *dormant* (Green 1986; de Bot 1992) may be an oversimplification which distorts the picture. If there is interference from both L1 and L2 in L3 production, but this interference is qualitatively different, rather than being distributed evenly over both languages, then we would have to assume that L1 and L2 are both active but in different ways. This is supported by two previous studies we carried out.

A pilot study of L3 word construction attempts in an adult learner of L3 Swedish, with L1 English and L2 German as background languages in L3 Swedish (Williams and Hammarberg 1994) showed that L2 German is the language predominantly used to supply material for word construction attempts. Here, we found interference from L2 German not only as regards stems but also as regards bound morphemes. As regards English, we found no interference with bound morphemes and only few instances of interference with stems. In this study we referred to the function of a language supplying material for word construction attempts as a *supplier* function, and the language or languages that have this function as *supplier languages*. Since Swedish itself can act as a supplier language, we further made a distinction between *intralingual supplier language* (i.e. when Swedish was used in L3 Swedish word-construction attempts) and *interlingual supplier language* (i.e. when another language was used in L3 Swedish word-construction attempts). Here, L2 German was the main interlingual supplier language. We referred to this role as *default interlingual supplier*. In what follows we will simply refer to it as *default supplier*. In the same study, we observed that L1 English was seldom used in supplier role, but rather was used as a tool to facilitate communication in the form of metalinguistic comments, asides, requests for help, and so on. We referred to this latter role as *instrumental*. German did not occur at all in this role.

In the early stages of L3 acquisition in the same subject, the influence of L2 German was not limited to the morphological and lexical level but was strikingly apparent also at the phonological level. In spontaneous speech, the subject's accent was initially strongly German, in terms of phonetic settings, prosody and voice quality. However, when asked to imitate L3 text segments read by a native speaker, L2 influence disappeared and

L1 English accent occurred. A further observation was that the strong L2 German phonological influence present in the early stages of the subject's L3 acquisition became less and less noticeable, so that after a period of one year, a gradual shift had taken place from a German to an English accent. When Swedish speakers listened to two recordings, one early recording and one recording a year later, and were asked to identify the native language of the speaker, there was general agreement that the first version was spoken by a native speaker of German while the majority choice for the second version was that it was spoken by a native speaker of English. This study of phonetic influence on the learner's speech will be accounted for in more detail in Chapter 3 below.

It is the main purpose of the present study to examine more closely the roles played by L1 and L2 in L3 acquisition by looking at the distribution of L1 and L2 over the various kinds of functions involved in non-adapted language switches. The aims of the study, then, are to see (i) to what extent L1 and L2 occur in the various types of language switches identified above, (ii) whether the roles of L1 and L2 change over time and (iii) what theoretical consequences these findings may have for polyglot and bilingual speech processing models.

2.5 DATA

2.5.1 Subject and method

The data presented here are taken from the project 'Processes in Third Language Acquisition', a longitudinal case study of an adult learner of L3 Swedish (Sarah Williams, henceforth SW). It will be noted that the subject is the same as the first co-author of this paper.[7] The material comprises recordings in the form of picture stories and conversations (with Björn Hammarberg, henceforth BH) which were carried out at approximately two-week intervals during the learner's first two years in Sweden. The data base comprises circa 37,000 word tokens produced by the learner (SW), and the working corpus for this study comprises 844 instances of non-adapted language switches.

SW's native language is British English and her L2s are German (fluent, near-native), French (advanced, non-fluent) and Italian (elementary, non-fluent). She studied French and German at university in England, spent one year in France during her university studies, and took an intensive one-month course in Italian at a language school in Florence at the age of twenty. After finishing university, she lived in Germany for six years and came to Sweden direct from the period spent in Germany. Recordings began immediately after SW's arrival in Sweden. At the beginning of the recordings, the learner was twenty-eight years of age. During the period of the recording (i.e. the first two years of her stay in Sweden) SW was working as a lecturer at the English Department at Stockholm University, a predominantly English-speaking environment. During this time she spent several weeks in both Germany and England, and received both German and English visitors at home in Sweden. Apart from this continued contact with German and English, her language environment was Swedish, which she acquired from her arrival through regular everyday interactions with Swedes.

Since the recordings were all carried out in interaction with BH, BH's language background is also relevant. BH's native language is Swedish and his L2s are English, German and French. He uses both English and Swedish as working languages, as is normal for academics in Sweden, and he studied German at university.

2.5.2 Coding

We identified four major types of non-adapted language switches, which we define here as being neither phonologically or morphologically adapted to the target language. The first we refer to as EDIT. This category contains terms which are used to introduce a self-repair (for example *no*, *sorry*) and also includes interactive feedback signals (for example *yeah*, *what*). The second is referred to as META, and comprises metalinguistic comments or questions. The third is referred to as INSERT, and comprises both attempts to elicit the L3 word from the interlocutor and also instances of codeswitching which appear to be used in much the same way as proficient bilinguals might codeswitch (i.e. sociopsychologically motivated codeswitching). All of these three categories we regarded as having

Table 2.1   Coding categories

Category			Description
EDIT	(1)	–	
META	(2)	COMMENT	
	(3)	FRAME	(containing EXPLICIT ELICIT)
INSERT	(4)	EXPLICIT ELICIT	(situated in FRAME)
	(5)	IMPLICIT ELICIT	(not situated in FRAME, but with rising intonation)
	(6)	NON-ELICIT	(no marked intonation)
WIPP	(7)	–	

pragmatic purpose. In addition to these, there was a fourth category which did not appear to have any identifiable pragmatic purpose. We referred to this category as Without Identified Pragmatic Purpose (shortened to WIPP). We believe that our WIPP category corresponds, at least in part, to what Poulisse and Bongaerts (1994) refer to as 'non-intentional language switches', although it will be noted that their category also includes our category EDIT. We prefer to use the term WIPP for three reasons: firstly, to avoid the inherent problems involved in attempting to use intentionality as a working criterion, secondly, to avoid the ensuing implication that our other three categories are 'intentional', and thirdly, to distinguish this category from EDIT. These categories were subcoded as shown in Table 2.1.

In all the examples given below, the items exemplifying the category in question are rendered in boldface.

EDIT

An item was coded as EDIT (1) if it was used as an editing term in a self-repair sequence, or used to facilitate interaction. Transcription conventions are given in Appendix 1 at the end of the book. English glosses are added to the examples where they facilitate comprehension.

(1) EDIT
    a. <der mann / **nee**> / mannen
        '<the man / **no**> / the man'   [0;1.11]
    b. i ett engelskttal-+ / <**no**> -talastelande+
        'in an english-speak- / <**no**> / -speaking country'   [0;5.15]

c. {<right>} här finns de en kvinna som städer
   '<right> / here is a woman who is cleaning' [1;7.10]

META

This group was divided into two subcategories. COMMENT (2) was used to indicate a comment on the communicative situation or on the L3 text itself.

(2) META COMMENT
   a. <I think it depends who I'm talking to> [0;0.14]
   b. B har du mycke kvar att göra på avhandlingen?
      S 'kvar' <does that mean 'problem'?>
      'B have you got much left to do on your thesis?
      S 'kvar' [= 'left'] < does that mean 'problem'?>' [0;1.11]
   c. <now it's working> [referring to the tape recorder] [1;2.10]

An item was coded as FRAME (3) if it constituted a frame for an explicit word eliciting attempt. Note that in the examples below, it is only the part of the utterance in boldface which has been coded as FRAME. The rest of the utterance is coded as INSERT (see next section).

(3) META FRAME
   a. <% whats 'to like'?> [0;0.22]
   b. <how do you say 'enjoy yourself'?> [0;0.29]
   c. <whats 'umschlag'?>
      'what's envelope?' [0;2.15]

INSERT

This group was divided into three subcategories. We regarded items as constituting EXPLICIT ELICIT attempts (4) if they were inserted into a frame, and as constituting IMPLICIT ELICIT attempts (5) if there was no frame but their intonation was marked (rising). If items occurred in the absence of either of these two conditions, they were coded as NON-ELICIT (6). Any items that were phonologically or morphologically adapted to the Swedish L3 were excluded. Examples of these are given below. Note that in Group 4, it is only the part of the utterance in boldface which has been coded as EXPLICIT ELICIT. The rest of the utterance is coded as FRAME (see previous section).

(4) EXPLICIT ELICIT
    a. <ho- how do you say 'they sound like'?>   [0;1.05]
    b. <what's 'to miss'?>   [0;4.03]

(5) IMPLICIT ELICIT
    a. sen har % har det här student % / <'looked at my watch'?>
       'then has % has this student % / <looked at my watch'?>'
       [0;1.05]
    b. han skulle kunna kanske % / <'to throw'?>
       'he could perhaps % / <'to throw'?>   [0;1.11]

(6) NON-ELICIT
    a. ja hade m- många <sachen>
       'I had m-many <things>'   [0;1.11]
    b. ja har sagt % till % till <fahrer> / till till mannen
       'I have said % to % to <driver> / to to the-man'   [0;1.05]

We also coded for whether or not such items were morphologically adapted to the utterance by using English or German morphological rules, respectively (for example conjugated verbs, plural marking, and so on). Since both L1 English and L2 German INSERT switches contained both morphologically adapted and morphologically non-adapted forms (in terms of English and German morphology, respectively), as well as non-decidable cases, this did not prove to be of direct relevance for our main research question, which was to identify differences in the behaviour of L1 and L2. Consequently, these results will not be discussed further.[8]

WIPP

WIPP switches were those which, in contrast to the other three categories, were regarded as being Without Identified Pragmatic Purpose. It was found to be typical of items in this category that there was immediate self-repair and/or abundant evidence from the preceding text that the corresponding items in the L3 were known to the subject.

(7) WIPP
    a. men alle personer <waren>/ % va va mycke hjälpfull
       'but all the people <were> / % were were very helpful'   [0;4.25]
    b. en tjuv % <mit> / med en nyckel

   '*a thief* % *<with>* / *with a key*' [0;2.15]

 c. den *<klei->* / den den lite pojken

   '*the <litt->* / *the the little boy*' [0;3.08]

A list of problematic areas within this categorisation together with a discussion of how we dealt with them can be found in the Addendum at the end of this chapter.

2.6 RESULTS

In what follows we will use the term *English corpus* and *German corpus* to refer to the collection of English and German language switches respectively. The discussion will centre around the English and the German corpuses. Items from other L2s will be discussed in more detail later. Table 2.2 gives an overview of the functional distribution of the languages.

  It will be seen that both L1 and L2 non-adapted language switches occur in L3 production. In general, it will be seen that there are approximately three times as many switches involving L1 English as there are involving L2 German, i.e. 74 per cent of all switches involved English, and 24 per cent involve German. Items from other L2s are, on the whole, negligible, constituting only 2 per cent.

2.6.1 EDIT

As regards the EDIT function, while more English is used than German, (70 per cent versus 29 per cent, respectively), this roughly reflects the general ratio of English and German occurrences.[9] Both languages occur here with roughly the same relation to their corpuses (9 per cent and 11 per cent respectively). There was only one instance of an EDIT term from another language.

2.6.2 META

As regards the META categories, both of the functions (COMMENT and FRAME) consisted entirely of English. Even in FRAMES in which German was used as the INSERT language, it was only English which comprised the FRAME.

Table 2.2 Overview of language switch distribution across categories for L1 English, L2 German, and other L2s

Category	L1 English				L2 German				Other L2s				Total (f)
	E (f)	E% all	E% E	E% cat	G (f)	G% all	G% G	G% cat	O (f)	O% all	O% O	O% cat	
(1) EDIT	57	7	9	70	24	3	11	29	1	–	6	1	82
(2) META COMMENT	73	9	12	100	–				–				73
(3) META FRAME	92	11	15	100	–				–				92
META TOTAL	165	19	26	100									165
(4) INSERT ELICIT EXPLICIT	133	16	21	89	16	2	8	11	1		6		150
(5) INSERT ELICIT IMPLICIT	75	9	12	73	25	3	12	24	3		19	3	103
(6) INSERT NON-ELICIT	187	22	30	68	78	9	37	29	8	1	50	3	273
INSERT TOTAL	395	47	64	75	119	14	57	23	12	1	75	2	526
(7) WIPP	3			4	65	8	31	92	3			4	71
TOTAL	620	74			208	24			16	2			844

KEY: (applies to German and Other L2 categories correspondingly)
E (f) shows the frequency.
E% all shows the percentage this constitutes of the entire corpus of switches.
E% E shows the percentage this constitutes of the English corpus of switches.
E% cat shows the percentage this constitutes of this particular category.

2.6.3 INSERT

As regards the INSERT functions, the occurrence of L1 English and L2 German roughly reflected the general ratio of English and German occurrences (3:1). Within the subcategories EXPLICIT ELICIT, IMPLICIT ELICIT and NON-ELICIT, both English and German were used most in the NON-ELICIT category (i.e. 'normal' codeswitching). In the ELICIT attempts, English occurred more in EXPLICIT ELICIT than IMPLICIT ELICIT, while the reverse was true of German. Indeed, as regards the EXPLICIT ELICIT category, 89 per cent of these were English and only 11 per cent German. This, however, is in some ways not surprising, as the FRAME into which such attempts are slotted is always English;

German in the EXPLICIT ELICIT position can be regarded as a case of double language switch. English EXPLICIT ELICIT constituted 21 per cent of the English corpus, while German EXPLICIT ELICIT constituted only 8 per cent of the German corpus. Apart from the EXPLICIT ELICIT attempts, however, English and German readings for what percentage this constitutes of their respective corpuses are very similar: 12 per cent and 12 per cent for IMPLICIT ELICIT attempts, and 30 per cent and 37 per cent for NON-ELICIT, i.e. 'normal' codeswitching.

2.6.4 WIPP

As regards the last category, WIPP, 92 per cent of all WIPP switches were German, with only 4 per cent from English and 4 per cent from other L2s. Table 2.3a shows the distribution of function words and content words in WIPP switches. It will be seen that function words far outnumber the content words.

These results support previous findings from the literature that it is predominantly function words that occur in WIPP switches. In the case of L3 production, these function words are predominantly from the L2. As regards similarity in form, an asterisk beside an item indicates that this is not similar to the L3 form. Table 2.3b gives the Swedish equivalents of all WIPP items. It will be seen from Tables 2.3a and 2.3b that not all of the types occurring as WIPP switches are similar in form to corresponding items in the L3 (cf. Vildomec 1963); twenty-seven out of seventy-two tokens are not directly similar in form.

However, even when there is no similarity, if we look at the larger unit and context in the near vicinity, in the majority of cases there are lexical and/or structural features from German in the larger unit. Although this sometimes results in correct Swedish, this is not always the case. Some examples of these are given below.

(8) vi vi måste har en = / <wir müss-> / vir m- vir måste
     har % fem fem **minuter** <vielleicht> % %
     *'we must have a / <we mus-> / we m- we must have % five
     five minutes <perhaps> % %'*
     [NB: Swedish *minuter* here has German pronunication,
     like German *Minuten*]   [0;0.22]

Table 2.3a   List of items in WIPP switches and their frequencies

Language	Function words		Content words	
	Type	Token	Type	Token
L1 ENGLISH	even	2		
	the *	1		
Total	2	3 (*1)		
L2 GERMAN	dann	7	klei- *	2
	er *	7	be-(wertet)	1
	und *	4	frei-(tag)	1
	ein	4	ging	1
	am *	3	gut *	1
	die	3	plötzlich	1
	mit	3	studen-	1
	so	3	typ-(isch)	1
	da	2	vielleicht *	1
	der	2	wein	1
	es *	2	wohnt-	1
	hier	2	ze-(hn) *	1
	das *	1		
	ihr *	1		
	konn-	1		
	ni-(cht) *	1		
	ob	1		
	waren	1		
	was	1		
	wer	1		
	wie *	1		
	wir	1		
	wir müss-	1		
Total	23	53 (*20)	12	13 (*5)
OTHER L2	un	2		
	comment *	1		
Total	2	3 (*1)		
TOTAL	27	59 (*22)	12	13 (*5)

* beside an item indicates that this is *not* similar to the L3 form.

NB: For reasons of clarity, the non-uttered completions of some of the interrupted lexical items, as apparent from their original context, are given in parentheses.

(9)   hon % gör också = % **det vad <er>** gör.
       'she % does also = % that which <he> does.'
       [German: *das was er macht.* Correct Swedish: *det (som) han gör*]
       [0;0.29]

Table 2.3b   List of items in wipp switches and similarity of their counterparts in Swedish

	Similar in form		Not similar in form	
	Item	Swedish equivalent	Item	Swedish equivalent
L1 ENGLISH L2 GERMAN	even	även	the	den
Function words	da	där	am	på
	dann	då	das	det
	der	den	er	han
	die	den	es	det
	ein	en	ihr	hennes
	konn-	kunde	ni-(cht)	inte
	mit	med	und	och
	ob	om	wie	hur
	so	så		
	waren	var		
	was	vad		
	wer	vem		
	wir	vi		
	wir müss-	vi måste		
Content words	be-(wertet)	bevärda (IL form: Sw. = värdera)	gut	bra
			klei-	lille
			vielleicht	kanske
	hier	här	ze-(hn)	tio
	wein	vin		
	frei-(tag)	fredag		
	ging	gick		
	plötzlich	plötsligt		
	studen-	student		
	typ-(isch)	typisk		
	wohnt-	bodde (cf. Sw. våning)		
OTHER L2s	un	en	comment	hur

It will be noted that in some of these cases, although the English equivalent is also similar to the Swedish item in twelve cases (namely *we must, what, how, we, there, could, ten, here, friday, little, typical, student*), it is nevertheless the German that is used. This indicates that while formal similarity in the lexical item itself or in the structural context of that unit may play a role in WIPP switches, since it is by and large only L2 items that occur, any effect of similarity is consequently restricted to L2.

2.6.5 Anomalous English

An interesting observation we found was that the kind of English which occurred in the category INSERT was sometimes anomalous, although no cases of this were found when English was used in a META function. Of a total of 395 English INSERT items, we found twenty-nine instances of anomalous English. These comprised three instances of slips of the tongue, sixteen instances of what we refer to as German-based English, eight instances of anomalous register/lexical usage, and two potential instances of transfer of training.

Slips

(10) % har ja tyck- / nej. <whats 'to though-' / 'to think
     of'>?   [0;4.25]
(11) nånting annat som som har = / <whats 'to discouraged' / <'to
     discourage'?>   [1;8.15]
(12) {s-} i stockholm centrum % = <i would b-> skulle jar+ =
     förköpa+¿ /<' i would sell'?>
     [0;1.05]

The three slips included two instances where the preterite form was combined with the infinitive form (Examples 10 and 11). In addition to these, there was one error in which a semantically related item *buy* was about to be used instead of the target item *sell* (Example 12). We did not consider these to be of further interest to our research question.

German-based English

Leaving aside the three slips mentioned above, in sixteen of the twenty-six remaining instances of anomalous English, there seemed to be strong German influence. This occurred only in cases of INSERT, and not in cases where English was used in META function. In these sixteen cases, English was not being used autonomously within its own language system, but rather was being used to render a literal translation of what the German would have been, if German had been uttered instead. German, then, seemed to be underlying the English. We refer to this as back-translation. All sixteen cases of back-translation are presented below.[10]

(13) <how do you say 'how father chr-'/ 'what father christmas looks like'?> 'hur santa claus ser ut'?
'*<how do you say 'how father chr- / 'what father christmas looks like'?>*
'*what father christmas looks like'?*'
[German: *wie der Weihnachtsmann aussieht.*][11]   [0;3.13]

An overt example of this strategy in action, so to speak, is given in the example below:

(14) <do do the swedes say 'f- finde ich' or <'i i i find' or 'i i th- i think' in the sense of 'ich finde' or 'ich glaube'?>   [0;1.05]

(15) ja finder¿ = ja finder¿ / <'i find'?>   [0;0.29]

The English back-translation (*I find*) of the German-based expression (*ich finde*) also occurs as complete, separate turntakes which actually adopt the pragmatic quality of what would have been in this case the German '*Finde ich.*'

(16) S   % de här italienska % utspråk / % uttal % liknar % svenska uttalet.
      B   jaha.
      S   <% i i find.>
      B   jaha. de e intressant.
      S   <i i find.> % da- dafür att % % . . .
      'S this italian accent is like the swedish accent.
      B really?
      S at least, I think so
      B yes. that's interesting.
      S yeah, I think so, because . . .'   [0;1.05]

Other examples of German-based back-translation are given below:

(17)   <whats *when*? 'if? 'if?>
       [German *wenn* can mean either *when* or *if*]   [0;0.22]

(18)   ja tror att ja har en en lite % <interference of> % från svenska nu
       *'I think that I have a a little % <interference of> % from Swedish
       now'*
       [German: Interferenz *von*. German *von* can mean either *of* or *from*.
       SW is talking about possible interference from Swedish in her
       English and German.]   [0;1.05]

(19)   <'many things to do'.>
       [German: *viele* Sachen. English: *a lot of* things.]   [0;0.29]

NB: This excerpt comprises part of a positive statement. *Many* tends to be used by native speakers of English mostly in questions or negative statements, rather than in positive statements, where *a lot of* is preferred; German L2 speakers of English, however, tend to use *many* also in positive statements.

(20)   men % andra personer % med med som ja har % talat¿ / <with
       whom ive sp- ive spoken>
       *'but other persons % with whom I've % spoken¿ <with whom
       I've sp- I've spoken>*
       [German: *mit denen ich gesprochen habe*. English: *who I've spoken to*.]
       [0;0.29]

(21)   S   ja hade mycke = {mycke} /
       B   {'tur'.}
       S   'tur'.
       B   'tur'.
       S   <'luck'>?
       'S   I had much = {much} /
       B   {*'luck'*.}
       S   *'luck'*
       B   *'luck'*.
       S   <*'luck'*>'
       [German: *ich hatte viel Glück*. English: *I was lucky*.]   [0;0.29]

(22)   (Talking about taking the tube to work, only ten minutes)
       S   % ja ja kan % % <'this way' 'auf' / = ho- how do you say
           'in this way'? 'auf'> /
       B   % 'så här'.

S 'så här'. så här kan ja spara¿ spara mycket % mycke timmar
'S % I I can % % <'this way' 'auf' / = ho- how do you say
'in this way'? 'auf'> /
B 'in this way'.
S 'in this way'. in this way I can save¿ save much % much hours'
[German: auf diese Weise. English: this means I can ... /
like this / by doing this]   [0;0.29]

(23) ja vilje % ta- / % säja % <'i had to find' or 'i i **must** find'>
'I wanted to % spe- / % say % <'i had to find' or 'i i **must** find'>
[German: ich mußte. English: I had to]   [0;1.05]

(24) <% how do i say 'i wouldn't have thought so'.
or 'i **wouldn't have imagined** that'?>
[German: das hätte ich mir nicht vorgestellt. English: I wouldn't
have thought so]   [0;1.05]

(25) <whats 'to % = **to say**' 'tell' 'relate' 'she tells him about'?>
[German: (jemandem etwas) sagen. English: to tell]   [0;1.11]

(26) och vet inte = vet inte vad han vad han / <'should = think'?>
'and doesn't know = doesn't know what he what he / <'should =
think'?>
[German: was er denken soll. English: what to do / what he should do]
[0;1.11]

(27) <'he cant get **away** from the chair.'?>
[German: er kann von dem Stuhl nicht weg. English: he can't
get **up** from the chair]   [0;2.09]

(28) de finns en = / ja. <whats 'a married **pair**'? 'married couple'?>
[German: ein **Ehepaar**. English: a married **couple**]   [0;3.00]

It will be noted that the above examples are typical of the kind of interlanguage utterances that native speakers of German make during L2 acquisition of English, i.e. the crosslinguistic effect of L1 German on L2 English is similar to the crosslinguistic effect of L2 German on L1 English during acquisition of L3 Swedish.

Register / lexical item

There were eight cases of English in INSERT function where, instead of the target word, a related word was chosen, but one from the wrong register, or a less common alternative, as in the list of examples given below. This was found to extend even to structural choice. We interpreted such cases as being of the same nature as the German-based English mentioned above, except that here, instead of being a back-translation of underlying German (i.e. German-based back-translation), the English seemed to be used to back-translate underlying interlanguage (IL) variants (IL-based back-translation), i.e. standard, unmarked, simplified forms.

ITEM PRODUCED	NORMAL TARGET

(29)   \<he wants her to do the same thing.
       he wants her to drink.>
       [0;0.29]
	to have a drink

(30) '\<die vänlichheit' 'friendliness>'. [0;0.29]	*they are friendly*

(31)   \<'he must be transported'
       \<'he must be carried'
       [0;1.11]
	he must be taken

(32)   \<how do you say 'she she manages it.'
       'she is s- successful.'? >
       [0;1.25]
	she succeeds

(33)   inte ska gör- göra \<babies>.
       'won't make \<babies>.'
       [0;9.09]
	so that they won't breed

(34) it must make some kind of [effect] [0;3.08]	*have*
(35) \<they shouldn't multiply.> [0;9.09]	*they shouldn't be allowed* *to breed*
(36) för att vatten % \<is delivered>. [0;9.09]	*for water to be delivered*

In all of the examples above, then, it would appear that the English is not used in a target-like fashion, but is moulded to fit in with the learner's interlanguage. In fact, it seems to be used to translate the exact form of the intended (but not yet produced) L3, or IL form. Here, one could posit that the form of the IL structure has already been decided upon, but cannot be executed in full because of the lack of the required lexical item in the L3. Here, English is used to 'render' the exact form sought after in the L3. English may be in the wrong register. This is the result of either simplification (cf. pidgin) or prototypicalisation. In the case of the latter, perceived transferability may play a role. Kellerman (1983) posits that direct transfer from L1 is more likely from elements in the L1 which are perceived as having a high acceptability probability; colloquial expressions are often avoided as are more marked constructions such as accusative-infinitive construction. If this applies to direct transfer, then presumably it applies too to substituting the intended L3 item with the actual L1 item itself, as in the case of IL-based back-translation.

Transfer of training

A last minor point to be made in this section regards possible transfer of training. Here, we found only two examples, both of which are what SW believes to be the result of the kind of vocabulary training she received during German lessons at school. In both of these examples, the English produced corresponds to the English terms used in the German class at school in order to make clear certain semantic distinctions in German lexical items that are not overt in English. If this is the case, then it would indicate that the transfer of training which is one of the five factors named by Selinker (1972) in the creation of a learner's interlanguage may have hitherto unsuspected longterm effects not only on the L2 but also on the L1 and on subsequent strategies for language learning.

(37) B <do you want to pay them because they don't complain? or % > /
      S <in order for them not to complain.>
      [English: *so that they won't complain.*
      Training: *damit sie . . .* = *in order for them*
                   sodaß sie . . . = *so that they* (result)]   [0;0.29]

(38) a. ja kände / <'i i got to know'?>   [0; 4.25]
      b. <how how do you say 'ken- kennenlernen' 'to get to know'>?
      [English: *I met them / to meet.*

Training: *treffen* = *to meet by prior arrangement*
                  kennenlernen = *to get to know*]   [0;5.15]

Although it might be objected that this kind of anomalous English may simply be a result of general L1 attrition in the subject, if this were the case, then we would expect similar phenomena to occur in the English used in the META category. No evidence of this was found. Also not surprisingly, we found no instances of German back-translation (i.e. English-based German items).

What these findings show, then, is that even when L1 English appears to be being used as an INSERT language, it may still differ from L2 German, in the sense of being used instrumentally, to translate German-based or IL-based items. Although these occurrences comprise only circa 7 per cent of the entire English INSERT corpus, the fact that they occurred at all shows that in these cases, English is being used in a special way. Also, as Ringbom (1987) points out, it is only when strategies result in non-target-like items that they are noticeable; in the rest of this section of the corpus, there may well be several other instances of this kind of L1 use which result, however, in target-like production of English, and are therefore impossible to identify.

2.6.6 Summary of results

A summary of the results for the English and German switches is given in Table 2.4. Both L1 English and L2 German occur in the EDIT category and also in the INSERT category. In sixteen cases, the English that occurred in the INSERT category appeared to be German-based back-translation, in eight cases, the English here appeared to be IL-based back-translation, and there were two possible cases of influence from transfer from German language training. In the META category, it was exclusively L1 English that occurred. In the WIPP category, it was predominantly (92 per cent) L2 German that occurred. Here, function words (twenty-three types, fifty-three tokens) outnumbered content words (twelve types, thirteen tokens). Twenty-five of the German WIPP switches showed direct similarity to the Swedish form, as opposed to forty-one which did not. Even where there was no similarity, a large proportion of the instances constituted

Table 2.4   Summary of results for L1 English and L2 German non-adapted language switches

Category	L1 English (%)	L2 German (%)
EDIT	70	29
META	100	0
INSERT EXPLICIT ELICIT	89	11
INSERT IMPLICIT ELICIT	73	24
INSERT NON-ELICIT	68	29
WIPP	4	92

part of a larger unit which was German-based (or where the Swedish construction and/or lexical items were similar to the German).

2.7 LONGITUDINAL ASPECTS

Tables 2.5–2.7 show the distribution of functions longitudinally over the corpus. In these tables, length of language exposure is shown in terms of years, months and weeks (i.e. 1;2.17 = one year, two months and seventeen days). The date of SW's entry into Sweden was taken as Day 1.

The longitudinal data show a decline over time in the frequency of language switches. As regards L1 English language switches (see Table 2.5), a general decrease in their occurrence appears after approximately eight months. Within the category INSERT, although ELICIT switches begin to decrease from this point onwards, NON-ELICIT switches, which represent 'normal' codeswitching, continue up until the end of the period studied. As regards German language switches (see Table 2.6), there is a marked decrease in their occurrence after roughly four months. This includes their occurrence in ELICIT function. They continue to occur sporadically in NON-ELICIT function (i.e. 'normal' codeswitching) for the rest of the first year but then do not appear in this function from 1;3.0 onwards. There is also a decrease in WIPP switches, the last observed instance of this category occurring at 1;5.15. Language switches involving languages other than L1 English and L2 German (see Table 2.7) are relatively scarce and occur more or less only during the first two and a half months.

Table 2.5   Longitudinal distribution of functions: L1 English

Trans. no.	Length of exposure	EDIT (1)	META (2)	META (3)	INSERT (4)	INSERT (5)	INSERT (6)	WIPP (7)	Total
01	0;0.14	4	4	1	1	1	10		21
02	0;0.22	2	5	6	10	6	6		35
04	0;0.29	6	6	4	6	11	9		42
05	0;1.05	9	12	10	14	20	28		93
06	0;1.11	5	10	7	13	10	12		57
08	0;1.25	1		3	3	2			9
09	0;2.09	1	2	9	10	2	6		30
10	0;2.15		1	3	4	1	3		12
11	0;2.22			2	2				4
12	0;3.08	7	6	9	12	1	13		48
13	0;3.13	2	5	7	9	3	10		36
14	0;4.03	2	1	4	6		2	1	16
15	0;4.25			1	2	4	2		9
16	0;5.08	1	1	2	2	1	1		8
17	0;5.15	2	2	5	6	1	3		19
18	0;6.07	1	5	1	1	2	9		19
19	0;6.26	2	1	2	3	4	17		29
20	0;7.18	1	3	4	5	2	5		20
21	0;8.03	3		3	5		2		13
22	0;9.09						5		5
23	0;9.28		1		1	1	5		8
24	1;0.30	1					3		4
25	1;1.18			1	1		2	1	5
26	1;2.10	2	5	3	8	1	2		21
27	1;3.00			1	2		4		7
28	1;5.10	1	1				2	1	5
29	1;5.15					1	9		10
30	1;5.28	1	1	1			8		11
31	1;6.16	1			1		3		5
32	1;7.10	1			1		1		3
33	1;7.25								
34	1;8.15		1	2	4	1	1		9
35	1;9.05	1		1	1		4		7
Total		57	73	92	133	75	187	3	620

Table 2.6 Longitudinal distribution of functions: L2 German

Trans. no.	Length of exposure	EDIT	META		INSERT			WIPP	Total
		(1)	(2)	(3)	(4)	(5)	(6)	(7)	
01	0;0.14	1			1	1	6	2	11
02	0;0.22	1				1	3	4	9
04	0;0.29					1	3	7	11
05	0;1.05	2			4	6	7	6	25
06	0;1.11	5			1	1	10	10	27
08	0;1.25				1	1	3		5
09	0;2.09	2			2	1	4	1	10
10	0;2.15	2			1	1		5	9
11	0;2.22					2		1	3
12	0;3.08	1			2	2	7	10	22
13	0;3.13				1	3	7		11
14	0;4.03				2	1	13	1	17
15	0;4.25	2					1	2	5
16	0;5.08						1	1	2
17	0;5.15				1			3	4
18	0;6.07						2		2
19	0;6.26					1	3	2	6
20	0;7.18	2				1		2	5
21	0;8.03						1		1
22	0;9.09						1		1
23	0;9.28						2	2	4
24	1;0.30	1					2	3	6
25	1;1.18	1				1			2
26	1;2.10						2	1	3
27	1;3.00	1							1
28	1;5.10	1						1	2
29	1;5.15	2						1	3
30	1;5.28								
31	1;6.16					1			1
32	1;7.10								
33	1;7.25								
34	1;8.15								
35	1;9.05								
Total		24			16	25	78	65	208

Table 2.7 Longitudinal distribution of functions: other L2s

Trans. no.	Length of exposure	EDIT (1)	META		INSERT			WIPP (7)	Total
			(2)	(3)	(4)	(5)	(6)		
01	0;0.14						2		2
02	0;0.22						1		1
04	0;0.29	1				1			2
05	0;1.05							1	1
06	0;1.11								
08	0;1.25				1	2			3
09	0;2.09							2	2
10	0;2.15						2		2
11	0;2.22								
12	0;3.08								
13	0;3.13						1		1
14	0;4.03								
15	0;4.25								
16	0;5.08								
17	0;5.15						1		1
18	0;6.07								
19	0;6.26								
20	0;7.18								
21	0;8.03								
22	0;9.09								
23	0;9.28								
24	1;0.30								
25	1;1.18								
26	1;2.10								
27	1;3.00								
28	1;5.10								
29	1;5.15								
30	1;5.28								
31	1;6.16						1		1
32	1;7.10								
33	1;7.25								
34	1;8.15								
35	1;9.05								
Total		1			1	3	8	3	16

2.8 Discussion

2.8.1 Role assignment

The fact that only L1 English occurred in the META category and almost only L2 German in the WIPP category provides strong evidence that there is differentiated distribution of L1 English and L2 German in non-adapted language switches. The occurrence of English in META function provides extended evidence of findings from Williams and Hammarberg (1994) that English is used for metalinguistic comments and asides, referred to as having *instrumental* role. It was found to be almost only German that supplied material for L3 lexical construction attempts (other than Swedish itself). We referred to German as having *default supplier* role. In the present study, with only few exceptions, it is almost only German that occurs in WIPP function.

We posit that WIPP switches are symptomatic of German being the *default supplier language.* This is supported by other data from the same subject showing German influence at various levels of language during the early stages of acquisition, not least at the level of structural and lexical planning. The notion that German, as default supplier, is 'online' all the time is supported by the apparent influence of German structure and lexical planning in some of the English INSERT utterances, where it is as if the English is being used for literal translations of underlying German. Indeed, the case of German-based back-translation would thus support the concept of German as default supplier language and also English as instrumental language.

Where might the assignment of these roles come from? We suggest that the assignment of instrumental role may be based on the speaker's identification with a particular language, modified by a knowledge of which languages are known to the interlocutor, and also on the interlocutor's identification of the speaker with a particular language and cultural sphere. We suggest that the assignment of default supplier role may be the result of interplay between four factors, namely, *proficiency, typology, recency* and *L2 status.* The language scoring the highest on all counts, so to speak, is the one which will be assigned default supplier role.[12]

Obviously, the effect of the various factors that determine the assignment of instrumental and default supplier role in each particular case will be subject to variation depending on the situation of the individual learner. It is a task for future research to explore this variation in detail. In the case under study here, English was used in everyday conversations between SW and BH during the early period of SW's residence in Sweden, a natural consequence of SW's English identity and the fact that both speakers knew English well. This would seem to motivate the use of English in the instrumental role in the Swedish conversations. Then, however, the question why German, and not English, assumes the default supplier role, remains to be explained. If we consider the four factors mentioned above, we may summarise in the following schema how they apply to SW's case (cf. the facts given in section 2.5.1 above):

	L1 English	L2 German	L2 French/Italian
PROFICIENCY	+	+	–
	(Native level)	(Near-native)	(Lower than German)
TYPOLOGY	+	+	–
	(Relatively close to L3)	(Relatively close to L3)	(Less close to L3)
RECENCY	+	+	–
	(Still in regular use)	(Still in occasional use)	(Not in current use)
L2 STATUS	–	+	+

This simplified schema points out some features that we think may be decisive in assigning the default supplier role to German in SW's case, given the fact that both English and German (and less so, French) were available to both SW and BH. Comparing L1 English and L2 German, we see that both obtain high scores (indicated here by pluses) for proficiency, typology and recency. SW could handle both languages with great ease. Both languages are relatively similar to Swedish. It could be argued that German is closer in vocabulary and means of word formation; on the other hand, this does not necessarily hold for lexical phrases or syntax. German scores high in recency, especially in view of the fact that SW moved directly to Sweden after several years' stay in Germany; English, too, was much used in and outside daily work. The decisive difference between English and German in this case appears to be in terms of L2 status. It seems to be this factor that crucially determines the default supplier role for German here, whereas English, despite high scores for the other factors, assumes a less prominent supplier role. But it is also clear that L2 status alone is not sufficient to motivate a default supplier role, as we can see when taking L2 French and Italian into account. These languages are outweighed by German in terms of proficiency, typological proximity to L3, and recency. Presumably, it is their L2 status which still allows them a minor role as supplier at the very early stage.

Although perceived typological similarity between L2 and L3 has been assumed to be the decisive factor in whether or not transfer takes place from L2 in L3 acquisition (Chandrasekhar 1978; Ringbom 1987; Vogel 1992) and a consideration of proficiency and typology has been pointed out earlier as being of potential importance to the workings of a bilingual speech model (de Bot 1992), what is new here is the incorporation of L1 versus L2 status itself into such a model. We believe that provided the factors of proficiency, typology and recency are at a sufficient level, L2s appear more likely to be activated than the L1 as supplier language during the early stages of L3 acquisition. Possible reasons for this include (i) a different acquisition mechanism for L1 as opposed to L2 and hence, in L3 acquisition, a reactivation of the same acquisition mechanism as was in previous L2 acquisition, which in turn reactivates other L2s and (ii) a desire to suppress L1 in the belief that this is inherently 'non-foreign' and thus that using a non-L1 and hence 'foreign' language would be a better strategy in acquiring another 'foreign' language. This last factor is based on various introspective comments by SW that were documented during the early period of L3 acquisition, to the effect that she did not want to sound English (cf. Chapter 1, p. 25). A pertinent question here is whether the fact that strong L2 German influence in the early stages of L3 acquisition, in terms of phonetic settings, prosody and voice quality, gives way to English influence (cf. Chapter 3) comes about as a result of activating the L2 or suppressing the L1, or both. This issue must, however, at present remain a matter for further speculation.

Once a language has been assigned default supplier role, it becomes the main source of crosslinguistic influence. It is this language that is activated in parallel to the L3, and may also underlie the production of L3 (along with the developing L3 inter-language). This L2 is the one used in the majority of interlingual lexical construction attempts up to the point at which proficiency in the L3 allows lexical construction attempts based predominantly on L3 itself and may also initially exert phonological/prosodic influence. It is because it is already parallel-activated that it acts as a default, such that (i) it is this L2 that then surfaces in WIPP switches, which are possibly due to performance factors such as level of attention, concentration, fatigue, and so on, and (ii) it is this L2 that underlies and influences the online production of even other languages (notably even L1) when used in an L3 context. As proficiency increases in the L3, so too does the independence of L3; both instrumental role and supplier role are gradually taken over by the L3. In our study, this can be seen by looking at the longitudinal data, which show a decrease in German and English occurrences. This is also supported by data from Poulisse and Bongaerts (1994) showing that non-intentional language switches (corresponding to our WIPP switches, which we posited as being symptomatic of default supplier role) occur less frequently in more advanced learners than in beginners.

It will be noted that Poulisse and Bongaerts' category 'non-intentional language switches' covers both our WIPP category and also EDIT category. What distinguishes EDIT from WIPP is that EDIT consists of interactive pragmatic elements which are not inte-grated into the content and structure of the ongoing utterance. As regards EDIT, again, both English and German are involved. Here, it is worth drawing attention to a neurological distinction in the processing of these two types of elements that has been found in crosslinguistic research on agrammatism in oral production (Menn and Obler 1990). Here, it has been shown that in agrammatism, there is a difference in the processing of content words, bound grammatical morphemes and free grammatical morphemes (func-tors). Content words tend to be preserved, bound grammatical morphemes are rarely omitted but can be substituted, and there is a high rate of omission in the majority of free grammatical mor-phemes. However, the kind of free grammatical morphemes which are discourse-controlled, such as fillers (for example *well y'know*) and sentence-initial conjunctions (for example *and, and then, and so*, etc.) were used abundantly. These latter correspond to the items found in our EDIT category. In other words, the free morphemes which could be regarded as resulting from the syntactic information present in a content-word lemma are those which are omitted in agrammatism, and occur in automatic switches to the L1 in L2 acquisition, and to the L2 in L3 acquisition (which could also be regarded as a kind of omission from the L3). On the other hand, the free morphemes which are discourse-controlled pragmatic elements, not dependent on syntactic integration, are those which are not affected in agrammatism and also those which, in switches, may occur from either L1 or L2. The existence of a different neurological mechanism in the processing of these two types of free morphemes may explain why WIPP may be symptomatic of default supplier, containing as it does almost exclusively L2 German elements, whereas EDIT is not, since it contains both L1 English and L2 German elements.

2.8.2 Relationship of our findings to models of bilingual speech production

Poulisse and Bongaerts' criticism of de Bot's (1992) model was twofold: firstly that if one language is selected already in the conceptualiser, then it is difficult to see how the other language could then be parallel-activated, and secondly, if this were somehow the case, it would, in the case of a polyglot, presumably lead to a potentially unlimited number of parallel-activated speech plans, which would be uneconomical. As regards the question of a shared or separate lexicon, Poulisse and Bongaerts opt for a shared lexicon with language tags. The solution of having language tags for items in a shared lexicon, however, cannot by itself explain why in the case of L3 acquisition it seems to be basically only one language which occurs in WIPP switches. Individual language tags per item may serve to identify items belonging to one or the other language system, but having a *default supplier* which is already more highly activated than other background languages would (i) be able to explain our WIPP switches and (ii) be more economical in the long run, in the sense of necessitating only one initial decision rather than several online decisions. Consequently, this means that (at least in addition to language tags), there must also be role assignment at a higher level.

Why should function words be more involved in WIPP switches than content words? Although any attempt to answer this question must at present be speculative, a possible explanation would be that function words are more automatised than content words. If the resources needed to block the articulation of a parallel-activated language are lowered, possibly due to factors such as tiredness (cf. Green 1986), then presumably those elements which are more automatised, i.e. those over which the speaker has less control, will stand more chance of slipping through the block (cf. Ringbom 1983).

At this point we would like to emphasise that at present, our model is a developmental one; the data presented here show that WIPP occurrences decrease over time. However, it has been observed (Stedje, personal communication)[13] that they may occur at a later period in situations of stress. SW's own informal observations of her later linguistic production support this. In addition, SW has observed that while such WIPP switches occur from L3 during L2 production when the speaker gets tired, they do not occur from L1 during L2 production, and only seldom from either L2 or L3 during L1 production. Taken together, these observations suggest that the notion of role assignment in the form of default supplier may also have relevance for a non-developmental steady-state model of language production in polyglots.[14] In the case mentioned above, L3 Swedish thus appears to act as default supplier for SW in her later use of L2 German. The latter observation given above also supports the notion that L1 is qualitatively different from a polyglot's other languages.

The assignment of default supplier role has consequences for Levelt's and also Paradis' (1987) contention that there is no theoretical difference between the different registers used by a monolingual speaker and the languages spoken by a polyglot. Our findings would suggest that there is in fact a distinction, since it is unlikely that such roles would be assigned to registers.

The existence of the posited role assignment is also in line with other findings from studies on language acquisition, where it has been shown that language learners in the initial stages of acquisition adopt the strategy 'one form, one function' (Andersen 1984). Polyforms and polyfunctions appear at a later stage of acquisition, when the learner is more able to cope with such phenomena. In the context of L3 acquisition, there appear to be different roles which can be kept separate by being assigned to different languages. This is in line with the principle of simplicity outlined above. It is in the context of L3 acquisition that the distinction between such roles, and hence perhaps ultimately their identification and definition vis-à-vis each other, becomes visible. In the case of L3, then, we see that L1 and L2 have different roles, which we have called *instrumental* and *supplier*. In the case of L2 acquisition, these roles must both be assumed by the only candidate available, namely L1, and overt distinctions between them collapse. In other words, the distinctions that are apparent in L3 acquisition are no longer apparent in the case of L2 acquisition, since L1 takes on both supplier role and instrumental role. Conversely, this also implies that there is a qualitative difference between the acquisition of a first L2 and other L2s.

A further point we would like to make here has to do with the problem of accounting for individual variation in language learning (for example Tarone 1982, 1985; Ellis 1985). Among the plethora of possible factors contributing to variability, very little attention has so far been given to the role of previously learned L2s. This picture is beginning to change, with studies comparing language learning in monolinguals and bilinguals (for example Mägiste 1986; Klein 1995). However, as pointed out earlier, such studies focus on issues pertaining to mental flexibility. The results of this study indicate that previously learnt L2s may play a role in individual variation in other ways. If it is predominantly an L2 and not the L1 that acts as a supplier language during the early stages of L3 acquisition, then simply looking to the learner's L1 (in conjunction of course with language universal factors and so on) will not give a full picture of the acquisition process (cf. Chandrasekhar 1978). We would stress, then, that a consideration of previously learned L2s may go some way towards accounting for the individual variation in learners that has been widely documented in the L2 literature, and even in cases of L2 acquisition in which there are no previously learned L2s, a consideration of the extent to which L1 is used in supplier role and in instrumental role may contribute to a better understanding of individual variation.

In conclusion, we support the principle behind de Bot's (1992: 2) statement that since every unilingual speaker has the potential to become bilingual, a basic model of speech production should be concerned with bilingualism, with an option to have a unilingual version. A related view is expressed by Cook (1992) who argues for the primacy of 'multicompetence' over 'monocompetence'. Both de Bot and Cook refer to the knowledge of *two or more* languages as a normal state, but do this in passing, limiting their own discussion to a bilingual L1-L2 situation. However, in the light of our L3 data, we would expand this: since every unilingual speaker has the potential to become multilingual, a basic model of speech production should be concerned with multilingualism, with options to have both bilingual and monolingual versions.

ADDENDUM: PROBLEMATIC CATEGORISATION, FROM SECTION 2.5.3

Borrowings and loan words

Borrowings and loan words occur particularly in cases in which the referent of the element in question exists in only one of the cultures in question. The question also arises as to whether pronunciation makes a difference: if an inserted element is pronounced with a Swedish accent, does this change its status? In the first example below, the items *good friday* and *easter monday* are very definitely English. These bank holidays also happen to exist in Sweden and have Swedish names (*långfredag* and *annandag påsk*), but this is cultural knowledge; many bank holidays are national only. Also, how should one classify items that presumably are international, such as *champagne*, which might well have been taken from the German although it also exists in both Swedish and English? And if SW believes that *sekt* is also an international concept, would this change its status as a quote?

Example: i england har har man också <good friday> och <easter monday>
            'in England we also have <good friday> and <easter monday>'
Example: man dricker champagne eller <sekt>.
            'they drink champagne or <sekt>'

If a borrowed item, although acceptable in Swedish, is not generally an established item in normal Swedish, we included this in the INSERT category. On the other hand, loan words which *have* been incorporated into Swedish were not included in the corpus.

Interlanguage or insert?

It was sometimes difficult to see whether an L2 item was being used with INSERT function or in an attempt to construct a word in L3. In the example below, the German form *gans* comes second in a sequence of word-construction attempts, but is however very similar to the other forms. In cases of doubt these were not included in the corpus.

Example: dom äter inte . . . ge- . . . gens . . . **gans** . . . jans . . . jens . . .
'*they don't eat . . . goo- . . . goose . . . goose . . . goose . . . goose*'

Particularly during the first few months, there were forty-three instances of items which, on the one hand, may have come from other languages, but were being used with the wrong meaning (for example *per*, from Italian, used with the meaning 'in'; *i*, from Italian, used as definite article plural; /e/, from either French or Italian, used with the meaning 'and'). Since these seemed to constitute part of the subject's IL, they were not included in the corpus of language switches.

Distinction between meta and insert non-elicit

Where a language switch occurred when the content of the L3 text actually included a meta comment, we assigned this to the category INSERT NON-ELICIT, our criterion for assignment to the META category being that the item does not constitute part of the content of the text, but is distinct from it.

Meta comment versus meta frame

Cases such as the one below were classified as COMMENT rather than FRAME, as it was not an explicit eliciting attempt (cf. What is the word for 'leg'?)

Example: <i do- i dont know what the word for 'leg' is.>

Meta versus edit

The borderline between META and EDIT categories was occasionally difficult. We classified non-referential comments such as *oh god* as EDIT and referential comments *oh god that's difficult* as META, although obviously the underlying meaning of both, when uttered as an expression of the speaker's difficulty with the text, is the same. The distinction we made between META and EDIT, then, rested on whether the utterance contained a referring term (META) or not (EDIT).

OK

OK is an international term, and in our material it is often used pragmatically at the beginning of a turntake, to register acknowledgement of the interlocutor's contribution or acceptance of a turn. Although it is international, we have regarded it as an English item since when it occurs in our material, it is uttered with an English accent.

Implicit elicit versus non-elicit

In cases of potential left-dislocation, it was difficult to decide if an item was embedded in a FRAME, whether it constituted an IMPLICIT ELICIT attempt, or whether it constituted simply a NON-ELICIT insertion. In such cases, we classified the operative utterance as FRAME if it contained anaphoric reference (for instance *that* in the example below).

Example: <'excited' 'aufgeregt' how do you you say that?>

NOTES

1. Note that the definition of what exactly constitutes content and function words is not resolved (cf. discussion in Muysken 1995). However, where this is relevant to a discussion of our

own data (Section 2.6.4), the reader will find a complete list of all the items we categorised in Table 2.3a.

2. There are several qualitative differences between the acquisition of a first L2 and a subsequently acquired L2, which ultimately means that the learner comes to the L3 acquisition task better equipped than was the case with the very first L2, in various ways. These include awareness of linguistic diversity, previous experience of certain strategies in L2 acquisition, and so on.

3. There are a handful of items, mainly adverbs, which are somewhat difficult to place. See Note 1. They are counted here as content words.

4. There may certainly be differences in the way language switching works in writing (as in the case of Ringbom's study) and in speech. We cannot, however, explore this point in the present context. As Ringbom points out, language switching is likely to be even more frequent in speech; thus, the passage we quoted from him goes on, 'In fact, it is probable that language shifts occur much more frequently in spoken than in written language, but even in the present written corpus complete shifts of Swedish function words make up a fair proportion (18 per cent) of the total number of lexical errors due to Swedish influence' (Ringbom 1987: 122).

5. Astrid Stedje, Department of German, Umeå University, Sweden.

6. Päivi Juvonen, Department of Linguistics, Stockholm University, Sweden.

7. We would like to point out that work on this study commenced more than three years after the final recording was made. During the time of the recordings, SW had not carried out any research on second or third language acquisition. Although there was some metalinguistic discussion and SW recorded introspective diary entries, at no point during the period of the recordings was there any discussion as to what kind of analyses would eventually be carried out on the data. The transcriptions were carried out by a research assistant after the last of this material had been recorded. Thus, the present authors do not feel that the data were in any way influenced by this or other potential studies at the time of collection and transcription.

8. Such results might, however, have a bearing on a model of codeswitching such as that presented in Myers-Scotton (1993), which posits that all embedded language items are morphologically adapted to the matrix language, although since our results are developmental and Myers-Scotton explicitly states that her model is not (1993: viii), this will not be discussed further here.

9. It should, however, be pointed out that the number of German EDIT terms would have been increased enormously if we had included the items 'ja' and 'also', which were abundant throughout the entire corpus. These were, however, not included as Swedish has two almost identical counterparts (*ja* and *alltså*) and it was not possible to ascertain what status these items had in our material, i.e. whether they belong to SW's interlanguage or whether they are indeed non-adapted language switches. However, regardless of whether these features themselves came from German or Swedish, the frequency of their ocurrence far exceeded that of native speakers of Swedish.

10. Some readers have suggested that some of these cases (nos 19, 20, 24) may not actually be so abnormal in English. They were interpreted in this way by SW, who insisted that she would not spontaneously use these forms in natural English discourse, and identified them as back-translations from German. I leave them as they stand, with this clarification. – BH.

11. NB: The fact that Swedish has a similar structure to German may mean that it is Swedish which is here being used as intralingual supplier. However, this is unlikely in view of the fact that German appears to underlie the other examples in this category.

12. This may provide an alternative explanation for Thomas' (1990) finding that Chinese/English bilinguals did not use their Chinese when learning Japanese; it may be not simply that English is their dominant language, as Thomas suggests, but rather that Chinese is their L1, and it is initially L2 that is activated during the early stages of L3 acquisition.

13. See Note 5.

14. We are using the term *default supplier* here within a developmental framework. We recognise that the role of a

parallel-activated language in a steady-state model may not necessarily fulfil the same functions as a parallel-activated language in a developmental model; we use the same term here, however, for the sake of simplicity, to denote the idea that even in a steady-state model, it may be the case that only one of a polyglot's other languages is parallel-activated.

Re-setting the basis of articulation in the acquisition of new languages: A third language case study

Björn Hammarberg and Britta Hammarberg[1]

3.1 INTRODUCTION

It has long been recognised that languages differ phonetically not only in their distinctive segments and prosodic features, but also in the characteristic ways in which the phonetic gestures are 'set', i.e. the *Artikulationsbasis, articulatory settings* (Honikman 1964; Laver 1980), or *phonetic settings* (Laver 1994). The discussion of *Artikulationsbasis* has a long history in the phonetic literature, especially from the point of view of the overall characterisation and contrastive description of the pronunciation of different languages (see Kelz 1971; Laver 1978; Jenner 2001 for historical accounts). Not least the great nineteenth-century phoneticians, such as Sievers, Viëtor, Sweet and Jespersen, emphasised and tried to portray cross-language differences concerning basis of articulation. In recent literature in English, the term *articulatory settings* (introduced by Honikman 1964) is widely used. Laver (1980, 1994) gives an extensive account of various dimensions and values of settings as features of people's habitual *voice quality*. Although he is primarily concerned with voice phenomena in the individual speaker, he also points out the relevance of settings for the characterisation of specific languages or language varieties (Laver 1994: 423ff). Regional variation of dialects, too, is characterised in part by differences in voice quality, an aspect which Elert has applied to Swedish dialect research (Elert 1984; Elert and Br. Hammarberg 1991). Likewise, voice can be an aspect of sociolectal variation (Esling 1978a, 1978b), and can function as a social marker of the speaker (Trudgill 1974; Laver and Trudgill 1979).

The articulatory settings have been identified with the speech rest position, or the neutral position of the speech organs. Gick et al. (2004) found significant differences between Canadian English and Québécois French speakers in an x-ray study of the vocal tract at the inter-utterance rest position, thus establishing that articulatory settings defined in this way can vary between languages. Extending this study, Wilson (2006) could corroborate these findings using a combination of ultrasound and Optotrak (optical tracking) techniques. He also investigated native-like English-French bilinguals and found that there was 'no unique bilingual-mode [interspeech posture], but instead one that is equivalent to the monolingual-mode [interspeech posture] of a speaker's currently most-used language' (2006: ii).

Settings have also been understood as the characteristic performance of the articulatory organs when they carry out the various types of gestures that are required by the phonology of the language. In the framework proposed by Laver (1980), the various types of settings which make up voice quality are grouped into *supralaryngeal* and *phonatory* (or laryngeal) settings, and the cross-cutting dimension of *tension* settings. In his partly modified terminology of 1994, he adds settings of *prosodic activities* as a further type. In Laver's definition (1994: 396), phonetic settings are 'any co-ordinatory tendency underlying the production of the chain of segments in speech towards maintaining a particular configuration or state of the vocal apparatus'. 'Settings give a background, auditory "colouring" running through sequences of shorter-term segmental articulations' (Laver 1980: 2). The settings thus interact with the gestures of the linguistically distinctive sounds and prosody and determine what has sometimes been called the idiomatic phonetic character of the language or variety in question.

The acquisition of a new language, then, involves not only the learning of a partly new system of distinctive speech sounds and prosody, but also the 're-setting' of the various aspects of voice quality in order to 'sound right'. The phonatory settings are probably that part which is least likely to be noticed spontaneously by language learners, and only few learners seem to attend to these in actual practice. As far as we know, phonatory settings have also been outside the scope of pedagogical books on foreign language pronunciation. The supralaryngeal and tension settings, on the other hand, were those aspects of articulatory basis that the early phoneticians commented on, as is clearly shown in Kelz's (1971) account. Such aspects are sometimes pointed out in language phonetics handbooks and pronunciation textbooks.

3.2 THE PRESENT STUDY

Our aim here is to present some pilot findings from a case study of an adult language learner who, already highly proficient in two languages, goes on to acquire a new language. We base this on the project 'Processes in Third Language Acquisition', conducted by Sarah Williams (SW) and Björn Hammarberg. Details on the project and on SW as the subject of this investigation were given earlier, particularly in Chapter 2, section 2.5.1. As mentioned there, SW was a native speaker of British English with a near-perfect command of German as a second language. She also had some second-language knowledge of French and Italian, but at a lower proficiency level than German. Since these languages do not seem to play a significant role in our present context, we will not be concerned with them here. In SW's case we are thus dealing with an established command of English and German, and the developing command of Swedish. We will use a terminology which identifies English as first language, L1, German as second language, L2, and Swedish as third language, L3.

Conversations and picture narrations in Swedish were tape-recorded at intervals right from SW's arrival in Sweden, and they, together with recordings in English and German, form the material for analysis. The recording sessions took place in an office-room, using a portable Marantz CP 230 tape recorder with an external table microphone. It should be pointed out that the wider project was actually not designed with the intention of making phonetic analyses, but rather with lexical and grammatical investigations in mind.

3.2.1 Cross-language variation of settings

The German basis of articulation is described by Wängler (1974: 167f) in terms of tongue, lip, jaw and velum settings. Generally, the articulation is more active than, for example, in English. In contrast to English, the dorsum tends to be kept in a convex shape, the apex seeks contact with the lower front teeth, and the tongue as a whole tends to be fronted, a setting which disfavours velarisation. The lips articulate forcefully both in spreading and in rounding, and rounding is connected with lip protrusion. The jaw and the velum, too, are rather active. Relatively strong overall muscular tension and high subglottal air pressure favour strong aspiration and fricativity. Non-gliding vowel qualities are also characteristic.

Differences between English and German articulations have been observed repeatedly in early phonetic literature; see Kelz (1971) for an overview. Thus, English articulations are generally more relaxed with less overall muscular tension and lower activity of the tongue and lips. The tongue is more lowered and retracted with a tendency towards a concave shape of the predorsum. There is no lip protrusion or active lip spreading. Vowel qualities tend to be gliding and less distinct than in German.

Contrasting German with Swedish, Korlén and Malmberg (1993: 42f) also point out the relative energy, tenseness and precision of German articulation and the absence of unclear, gliding vowel qualities in German. They give a detailed account of the differences in lip articulation, stressing the lip protrusion and the 'horizontal' rounding movement in German in contrast to the less energetic 'vertical' rounding in Swedish. Swedish has two series of rounded vowels, one with a type of lip protrusion and one without, but both are different from the German type. More than in Swedish, the lip-rounding of German vowels tends to spread to adjacent consonants. Another difference is the stronger tendency in German to realise unstressed /en/ as a syllabic nasal.

Swedish, then, has generally less forceful articulations than German, but less relaxed than English. Swedish does not share the English tendency toward a retracted, low or neutral tongue position. Hence, unlike English, unstressed vowels are not neutralised to shwa, short (lax) vowels are less lax, apical stops are more fronted, and there is no velarisation of /l/.

3.2.2 Second language performance

We played a recorded passage of *SW's German speech* from her first month in Sweden to three native North German listeners (teachers at the German Department of Stockholm University) to obtain their impressionistic judgments. Two of them identified her as a northern German without any specific local dialect, and did not think of her as a foreigner. Some minor peculiarities were observed. The third listener said that she could be 'an American, speaking excellent German, sounding like a German, or possibly a German who has lived in America'. This judgment was based on the pronunciation of sound segments at some specific places on the tape, and not on the general colouring of her speech. Being asked, all three native judges said they noticed nothing remarkable about SW's basis of articulation or voice quality. Considering that significant differences between English and German articulation are indeed attested in the phonetic literature, we may thus conclude that, by and large, SW was able to switch successfully between English and German settings.

3.2.3 Third language performance, early and later stage

To obtain reactions on *SW's Swedish speech* at an early and later stage of development, a picture story narration was played from the tape to native Swedish listeners. The same story, *Hunden* 'the dog', had been recorded on two occasions, during the first session, a few days after SW's arrival in Sweden (*Hunden 1*), and then a year later (*Hunden 2*); both transcripts are shown in Appendix 2. The task for the Swedish listeners was to identify the native language of the speaker (without being told that *Hunden 1* and *2* were spoken by the same person). There was general agreement that *Hunden 1* was spoken by a German. As for *Hunden 2*, the judgments varied more, but the majority choice was English. There were various comments on sound segments, intonation contours and occasionally also voice quality.

We (the present authors) have listened separately to SW's narrations of *Hunden*. Tables 3.1 and 3.2 show some conspicuous features which both of us have noticed in her two versions:

As can be seen in the tables, there are several details in SW's speech which point to a predominant influence from German in *Hunden 1* and English in *Hunden 2*. The effects of characteristic

Table 3.1   Features of sound segments noted in *Hunden 1*

Swedish target	Examples in data	Realisation by SW	Apparent crosslinguistic influence
[ɪ]	v<u>i</u>ll, t<u>i</u>ll	more lax-open [ɪ̞]	English/German
[ʉ̟ː]	h<u>u</u>set	German-type rounded, tense, back [uː]	German
[ɒː]	h<u>a</u>, j<u>a</u>	less retracted, unrounded [aː]	German
[s] inter-vocalic	hu<u>s</u>et, lä<u>s</u>er	voiced [z]	German
[ɹ] post-vocalic	ä<u>r</u>, ta<u>r</u>, gå<u>r</u>, framfö<u>r</u>, springe<u>r</u>, läse<u>r</u>	uvular approximant [ʁ], or vocalised [ɐ]	German
[ən]	hund<u>en</u>, tidning<u>en</u>	syllabic nasal [n̩]	German

Table 3.2   Features of sound segments noted in *Hunden 2*

Swedish target	Examples in data	Realisation by SW	Apparent crosslinguistic influence
[ɪ]	finns, t<u>i</u>ll	more lax-open [ɪ̞]	English/German
Vowels, unstressed	kast<u>a</u>r, fortfar<u>a</u>nde	shwa [ə]	English
[t], [d]	<u>t</u>ill, li<u>t</u>e, sis<u>t</u>a, e<u>tt</u>; <u>d</u>e, bil<u>d</u>en	retracted [t̠], [d̠]	English
[l] postvoc.	ti<u>ll</u>, bi<u>l</u>den, sjä<u>l</u>	slightly velarised [ɫ]	English
[ɹ] postvoc.	hä<u>r</u>, se<u>r</u>, sitte<u>r</u>, framfö<u>r</u>	more prominent apical approximant	English

German and English articulatory settings are apparent here. There is a general colouring of SW's speech which appears German-like in *Hunden 1* and English-like (for example in vowel qualities) in *Hunden 2*. In *Hunden 1* there is a tense quality in the stress and intonation patterns of stressed two- and three-syllable words, such as *hunden, huset, tidning, tidningen, framför*. This characteristic is absent in *Hunden 2*. The voicing of intervocalic /s/ (*läsa, huset*) and the uvular realisation of /r/ (*är, tar, går* etc.) in *Hunden 1* – clearly German influence, although more properly attributed to the phonological rule system than to articulatory settings – has also disappeared in *Hunden 2*.

3.2.4 Phonatory re-settings?

In order to examine aspects of *phonatory settings*, we tried acoustic measurements on four extracts of SW's speech, namely, a passage in *English*, a passage in *German*, as well as *Hunden 1* and *Hunden 2*. The methods we applied here have also been used earlier by Elert and Br. Hammarberg (1991) in analysing phonatory qualities of Swedish dialects. Fundamental frequency distribution analysis (*Soundswell*, Ternström 1990) was used with the hypothesis that, firstly, we would find differences in mean Fo frequency and Fo range between the English and German extracts, representing possible differences in SW's setting of fundamental pitch level for English and German. Secondly, if this turned out to be the case, we hypothesised that it would also be reflected to some extent in a difference between *Hunden 1* (more German-oriented) and *Hunden 2* (less German-oriented). However, the measurements on these short extracts neither confirm nor rule out such differences.

We also ran waveform perturbation measurements on the same four extracts, in order to capture possible voice quality characteristics such as vocal fry and roughness, which might be correlated with low pitch. This yielded low values for perturbation throughout, within normal range.

The results from these attempts to measure phonatory qualities are thus so far inconclusive. It may be either that there were in fact no systematic differences in SW's speech, or that the recordings were not acoustically good enough for the purpose. We do not find, however, that the inconclusive outcome at this point argues against using acoustic measurements in trying to explore how language learners handle phonatory settings. We would rather encourage further research along these lines. Even firm results to the negative would be valuable. It would, for instance, be interesting to find out if particular language learners (or most learners?) tend to re-set supralaryngeal articulations while leaving their phonatory settings unaltered in the new language.

3.2.5 Task-related variation

During the first recording session, SW also read aloud two short passages from a Swedish beginner's textbook. This was arranged as two different types of task. The first text was read out by a native Swedish speaker in segments of a few words at a time which SW then immediately repeated (the '*read-after-me*' task). The second text was read by SW alone without a model (the '*read-on-your-own*' task). There is a clear difference in character between the two readings. The *read-after-me* text shows various imitative attempts, some more English-like, some more German-like, some neither, but the overall character appears less German than English. To mention a few observed details, Swedish [ɒː] (*sta̲d̲*) occurred more retracted-rounded, approaching [ɔː]. Swedish [ç] (*k̲ök̲*) was rendered rather like English [ʃ]. The /r/-sounds were mostly realised as an apical trill [r] or approximant [ɹ] (*r̲um, br̲a, bar̲a, tor̲get*), but occasionally uvular [ʁ] or vocalised [ɐ] (*tr̲ettiofem, år̲, Lundber̲g*). (A complication in the case of /r/ was that the model Swedish speaker happened to be a 'uvular R' speaker, whereas the other Swedish researcher present on the occasion was an 'apical r' speaker.)

The *read-on-your-own* passage shows a markedly stronger German character. Here are some noted observations: Swedish [ɒː] (*la̲ga, ma̲t*) occurred with a relatively fronted, unrounded quality, like German [aː]. Swedish initial prevocalic [s] was rendered alternatingly as [s] (*s̲äng, s̲å*), or voiced [z] as according to German phonology (*s̲ätt, s̲äng, s̲ängen*). Syllable-final obstruents were devoiced (*bor̲d̲, vär̲d̲, bre̲d̲, ta̲vl̲or*) as in German. The /r/-sounds this time were uvular or vocalised throughout (*r̲um, dr̲aperi, dör̲ren, vär̲d, mattor̲, framför̲*, etc.).

There is a strong overall German colouring in this second passage. Laver (1980: 5) uses the notions of figure and ground to describe the relationship between the linguistically functioning features of sounds and the articulatory settings. This metaphor seems very relevant here: the particular sound qualities we have noted figure against a ground of articulatory settings which is characteristically German oriented in the second text passage.

3.3 DISCUSSION: THE RE-SETTING PROCESS

SW's ability to switch between English and German settings is the result of an articulatory re-setting process in second language acquisition. Only the result is of course visible now, not the developmental process which led up to it.

But in the way SW tries to cope with Swedish as a third language, we can observe certain aspects of how the articulatory settings are handled in the process.

SW's strong tendency to rely initially on her German settings rather than her English ones is obvious both from the *Hunden 1* and the *read-on-your-own* data. She stated at an early stage that she did not want to 'sound English' when speaking Swedish. Obviously she felt freer to rely on the system of another non-native language that she had available, when trying to approach Swedish pronunciation. One furthering factor was undoubtedly that she could speak German so easily and thus it was very fresh in her mind. But still it is remarkable that a second language so strongly outweighs and even suppresses the influence of the native language in this situation.

However, this dominance of L2 over L1 in incipient L3 acquisition is not unique to the pronunciation domain. SW also made much more use of German than English as an *external supplier language* in her frequent attempts to construct hypothetical Swedish lexemes during the early period; we will elaborate on this in the following chapters. Further evidence for SW's initial reliance on German comes from the so-called 'WIPP' ('Without Identifiable Pragmatic Purpose') switches which were dealt with in Chapter 2, i.e. language switches of an apparently automatic kind, which mostly affect grammatical function words. Whereas other, pragmatically purposeful types of switches that also occur are true code-switches which do not constitute attempts to speak Swedish, the WIPPs are seen to arise during SW's utterance formulation in Swedish. In contrast to the various 'pragmatic' switches which in most cases involve English, the WIPPs are usually switches into German. They suggest that L2 German was often co-activated during SW's formulation work in Swedish in the early stages.

It is likely that a combination of conditions favoured SW's reliance on German articulatory settings in her acquisition of Swedish, such as her high proficiency and her easy and recent use of German. These factors could in principle quite as well apply to English and favour the use of English settings, but the fact that German settings were the ones that were actually used points to a *foreign language effect* (Meisel 1983) that arises due to the *L2 status* of German (cf. Chapter 2 above) as a decisive factor furthering German in SW's case. The L2 status effect has been discussed by several authors; cf. for example De Angelis and Selinker (2001); Hammarberg (2001); Cenoz (2001, 2003b, 2005); Bardel and Falk (2007). For SW, both Swedish and German were non-native languages. Apparently, a similar mechanism for acquiring and accessing later languages, as opposed to first languages, tends to make a prior L2 easier to activate when acquiring a new language. This also involves an aspect of attitude. As mentioned above, SW reported that she did not want to 'sound English' when speaking Swedish; the support from another, familiar non-native language could free her from the dependence on L1. Clearly the use of German articulatory settings and sound qualities have been helpful in SW's case in avoiding some unwanted aspects of L1 influence, such as strongly diphthongal vowel qualities.

The factor most often cited as causing crosslinguistic influence in the L3 acquisition process is the typological similarity between L3 and a background language, L1 or L2. Many L3 acquisition studies have furnished support for typological similarity as a major factor; for relevant discussion, cf. Cenoz (2001, 2003b). In SW's case the (perceived) degree of similarity of L1 English and L2 German to L3 Swedish comes in focus. All three languages are obviously rather close. The typological similarity factor may have played a significant role in furthering German influence in the lexical area, but less so in connection with WIPP switches which seem to occur irrespective of any crosslinguistic similarities. In the case of SW's articulatory settings the typological similarity factor can at most have played a 'passive' role in that German settings and phonology are not drastically alien to Swedish, in which case they would probably have been avoided. It can hardly be maintained that North German articulatory settings are significantly more similar than British English settings to the pronunciation of Swedish. Note also that the German influence on the articulatory settings occurred right from the start, at the very initial stage when SW had had few opportunities to evaluate similarities and differences between Swedish and the two background languages. Thus the conclusion must be that the relative typological similarity of L1 and L2 to L3, which admittedly has proved to be an important factor with other learners and language constellations, especially in the lexical and grammatical domains, is less decisive for SW's articulatory settings in L3 than the effects of L2 status.

As SW got more acquainted with Swedish and her skills became automatised, her reliance on German gradually decreased. This is apparent in the lexical and codeswitching material just mentioned, and *Hunden 2* exemplifies a stage where this process in the phonetic domain has gone quite far. When the German articulatory settings no longer prevail, there is scope for some remaining phonetic influence from English, as evidenced by *Hunden 2*. The phonetic domain differs in this respect from the domains of lexis and utterance organisation where no phase of increased L1 influence emerges when L2 influence disappears. We suggest that this difference can be accounted for by the fact that articulatory patterns have a basis in neuro-motor routines that have been established according to L1 requirements and are difficult to control or modify at will. It thus seems that influence from L1 on articulatory settings is a basic *constraint* on articulation which tends to be persistent in language learning, whereas the reliance on L2 settings is a *coping strategy* which the learner resorts to at an initial stage when the phonetic form of L3 is too unfamiliar to master, and abandons when proficiency in L3 increases. This coping strategy is seen to override the basic constraint temporarily.

The fact that the use of L2 settings is conditioned by capacity factors is evidenced in the two different reading tasks. It is natural that SW's speech performance in the *read-after-me* task should be input oriented and imitative, and of course facilitated by the model, whereas the reading without a model forces the beginning learner to rely on prior knowledge.

It is interesting to note that SW's reliance on L2 settings tends to colour her pronunciation in the L3 in a global way, extending continuously over longer stretches of speech, rather than causing a local effect on particular words or parts of words. This should in fact be expected from the definitions of settings given above, and from the way the workings of settings are described in the phonetic literature (cf. for example Laver 1980, 1994). Honikman (1964) introduces the metaphor of a 'gear' to describe how the switching to the articulatory settings of another language can function for language learners. In her language classes, expressions like 'in

English gear', 'You're out of gear', could help the students observe the appropriate articulatory settings as a basis for their pronunciation. Similarly, when SW speaks German, and Swedish initially, her use of German settings appears to function like a 'gear', a switch into the overall use of the German system of settings. In her subsequent Swedish development this 'gear' is then modified and replaced by approximations to the norms of the target language and the lasting traces of L1 influence.

NOTE

1. Britta Hammarberg is Professor (now Emerita) of Logopedics at the Karolinska Institute, Karolinska University Hospital Huddinge, Sweden. Her main research interest is clinical voice research.

CHAPTER 4

The learner's word acquisition attempts in conversation

Björn Hammarberg

4.1 INTRODUCTION

For language learners, spoken interaction with target language speakers not only has the function of achieving communication, but also has an acquisitional role in providing opportunities for the learners to expand their interlanguage, chances which different learners will exploit to varying degrees. Formulation attempts furnish occasions for a learner to search, establish, practise and consolidate new expressions, either in spontaneous use in passing or in active cooperation with the interlocutor. Especially the latter case, where the learner appeals to the target language speaker, offers the researcher a possibility to study the acquisitional attempts in detail. Our focus here will be on lexical items. The purpose of the article is to describe and discuss the attempts by one particularly active learner to elicit and try out new vocabulary in conversations with a native speaker.

The study of lexical acquisition processes in language production of course has parallels on the comprehension side. Thus learners' vocabulary expansion by reading has been studied extensively (for a review of this research, see de Bot, Paribakht and Wesche 1997). Haastrup's (1985, 1987, 1990, 1991) detailed studies of the process of lexical inferencing provide a close-up view on how learners try to find out the meaning of encountered unfamiliar words, focusing especially on how the learners reason about the words and what knowledge they bring to bear on the task.

The (largely) complementary relationship between lexical inferencing and lexical search during formulation can be expressed in the terms of Levelt's (1989, 1993) speech production model. In this framework the entries in the mental lexicon are viewed as the association between a *lemma* part, containing the word's semantic and syntactic information, and a *form* or *lexeme* part which gives the corresponding phonological shape, or set of shapes. Thus whereas (for a language learner) lexical inferencing is a matter of establishing a lemma for a given lexical form, lexical search starts with an intended (tentative) notion for which a lemma is expected to exist in the target language, and the task is to arrive at an appropriate lexeme.

The particular type of exchange in the course of learner–native speaker conversations where the learner elicits and receives elements in the target language from the native interlocutor has been discussed by several researchers (De Pietro, Matthey and Py 1989; Py 1990; Vasseur 1990; Bartning 1992; Bozier 2005, all dealing with L2 acquisition of French). The point they have made is that such exchanges can be viewed as *séquences potentiellement acquisitionnelles*, i.e. they may constitute crucial moments in the learner's acquisition of target language structure. Py (1990) describes such sequences as typically consisting of (i) an elicitation attempt by the learner (Py's French term: *sollicitation*), (ii) a phase where the target expression is given by the interlocutor (*donnée*), and (iii) a phase where the learner shows that he or she has received the target expression (*prise*). Whereas De Pietro et al., Py, and Vasseur stress the cooperative interaction between the learner and the interlocutor and particularly focus on the active role of the latter, our concern will be more with the learner's pre- and post-reception activity, which appears to be particularly elaborate in the case of our present learner.

4.2 THE PRESENT STUDY: SOURCE OF DATA

The examples to be presented here are taken from the longitudinal corpus of recorded conversations collected within the project 'Processes in Third Language Acquisition' which was conducted jointly by the present author (BH) and Sarah Williams (SW). The learner who was the subject of our case study was SW herself.

Recapitulating facts about the project mentioned in the previous chapters, English was SW's L1, German her main L2, along with the 'other L2s' French and Italian, and Swedish was in this situation her L3. She was a linguist by profession, having studied languages in England and done research in Germany on child bilingualism, and was now taking up a teaching position at Stockholm University. However, she did not enroll in an organised course to learn Swedish, or devote herself to grammar reading, but relied on acquiring the language in her work and daily life. In order to document her gradual development in Swedish, we – SW and BH – started upon her arrival in Sweden to audio-tape conversations between the two of us regularly, an activity which we carried on for two academic years. This yielded an oral text corpus consisting of interviews, discussions and picture narrations and comprising 55,000 word tokens, of which 37,000 were produced by the learner (SW). The linguistic analysis of the material began only after the entire corpus had been collected.

4.3 WORD ELICITATION UNITS

In these recorded conversations, there are passages where the learner elicits words from the interlocutor which she needs in the conversation. It is mostly lexical items, mainly content words, which are sought in this manner, even if SW occasionally also elicits grammatical forms and constructions. We will focus here on the lexical area and study the passages in the recordings where the learner makes efforts to acquire a particular target word. Each such passage will be referred to here as a *word elicitation unit (WEU)*. WEUs for 301 different target words were found in the corpus, and since some of these words were elicited more than once, there is a total of 374 WEUs.

Example (1) illustrates the basic structure of a WEU. (Cf. the key to the transcription in Appendix 1 at the end of the book.)

(1) S hon kommer på % på % **lörsda¿ lörsda¿**.
     B 'på **lörda**'.
     S 'på **lörda**'. mhm. % inte inte de här % **lörda** men % en en veckan / en vecka % för- försent.

'S she'll come on % on % lörsda¿ lörsda¿.
B 'on saturday'.
S 'on saturday'. mhm. % not not this % saturday but % one one
   week / one week % la- later.   [0;1.05]

The criteria that we require for recognising a *word elicitation unit* are (a) that the learner shows some activity in eliciting a target word, and (b) that the interlocutor supplies the word, or at least approves a form suggested by the learner. The learner's word-searching initiative is essential here. The target is not simply supplied as a correction initiated by the interlocutor. It seems obvious that when these two criteria are met, there is evidence for an acquisitional attempt. The learner clearly uses word elicitation both as a communication strategy and as a learning strategy. In most cases, the learner will also acknowledge the reception in some form, by a repetition, a *yes* answer, by using the word actively, and so on.

It will be apparent at this point that WEUs correspond in their general structure to the potentially acquisitional sequences posited by De Pietro, Matthey and Py. There are, however, some differences in emphasis and perspective between their approach to the phenomenon and the one taken here. First, we are dealing here with lexical items only (which is of course only a practical limitation). Second, while it is understood that the WEU is basically an interactive event, our primary concern is with the learner's activity within this interactive frame. Third, both the WEU as a word-searching event (a token unit) and the target word as a lexical item (a type unit) will be given attention. Finally, WEUs may be 'acquisitional' in a short-term or a long-term sense. We will first explore the act of short-term acquisition that each WEU constitutes by definition, and then touch upon the possible long-term acquisitional effect which is suggested by the term *séquence potentiellement acquisitionnelle*.

Example (1) above illustrates a simple, straightforward case of WEU in which S's first turn constitutes what will here be referred to as the *pre-reception phase*, B's turn the *reception point*, and S's second turn the *post-reception phase*. We will look in turn at these successive parts that make up the WEU. Consider the following additional examples:

(2) S % ja ja va % mycke '<surp- surprised>' / '<über->' / öv-
        över- överräscht / över- överraschade.
     B 'du va mycke överraskad'.
     S överraskad (B: JA) att han har fö- förstått (B: MHM) % att han
        fer- ferstått vad ja % hade % hade säjat.
     'S % I I was % very '<surp- surprised>' / '<über->' / öv- över-
        överräscht / över- överraschade.
     B 'you were very surprised'.
     S surprised (B: YES) that he has un- understood (B: MHM) % that
        he has und- understood what I % had % had said.'
     [German überrascht = 'surprised']   [0;1.05]

(3) S ja tycker om % lären / lä- lärare. ja {tycker} /
     B {du tycker} om att vara lärare. {eller} /
     S {ja} ja ja tycker om % att lärare / att lära. <i like teaching.>
     B ja. % du menar alltså att 'du tycker om % att vara
        lärare'. eller 'du tycker om att undervisa'.
     S 'undervisa'.
     B ja.
     S jaha. ja tycker+ om att undervisa.
     'S I like % lären / lä- lärare. I {like} /
     B {you like} being a teacher. {or} /
     S {yes} I I like % att lärare / att lära. <I like teaching.>
     B yes. % you mean then that 'you like % to be a teacher'.
        or 'you like to teach'.
     S 'teach'.
     B yes.
     S well yes. I like to teach.'
     [German lehren = 'teach'. Swedish lärare = teacher]   [0;0.22]

(4) S han ändra % = det här.
     B mh håret / frisyren.
     S frisyren å % ågen¿ (B: {JAHA}) / {ögen¿}.
     'S he changes % = this.
     B mh the hair / the hairstyle.
     S the hairstyle and % the eyes¿ (B: {YES}) / {eyes¿}.'   [0;0.29]

(5) S ja tycker inte om att % att har % / <what's 'feeling'?>
     B 'känsla'.

S att har **känslan** % att j- / att % de är mycke tråkig (B: MHM) %
för personerna när ja % be- berädda nånting.
'S *I don't like* % *having* % / <*what's 'feeling'?*>
B *'feeling'.*
S *having the feeling* % *that I-* / *that* % *it's very boring (B: MHM)* %
for the persons when I % *te- tell something.'*   [o;2.15]

(6) S målar+¿ / målen¿ målen¿ må- /
B 'målaren'.
[English: *'the painter'*]   [o;0.29]

The *pre-reception phase* of a WEU contains the learner's elicitation
attempts, often combined with tentative word constructions, as in
the examples here. Various types of elements in the learner's utterances may function as signals of elicitation:

— iteration of a form (ex. (1) above);
— metalinguistic questioning intonation on a tentative form, as
  indicated by '¿' in ex. (1);
— gradual buildup of a form by partial iteration, as in (2) and (3):
  öv- över- överräscht; lä- lärare;
— self-repair, marked here by '/', as in (2) and (3);
— language switch, marked here by '< >';
— a noticeable empty pause ('=') and/or a pause-filling sound
  ('%'), as seen in example (4);
— a deictic indication, as in (4): *det här* 'this', where the learner
  points to her hair;
— an explicit question to the interlocutor to supply the intended
  word, as in (5);
— turn interruption, as in (6) (turn ending with '/' after an incomplete utterance).

There is a variation in explicitness between these different types of
elicitation signals. *Language switches* and especially *overt questions*
are obviously explicit means which form clear cues for the interlocutor. At the other end of the scale are such elements as *pause*,
pausefiller, iteration and *gradual buildup*. Being normal elements of
utterance production they occur freely even outside WEUs. They
never achieve elicitation by themselves, but only in combination

with more explicit signals. But then they undoubtedly contribute
to the impression that the learner is searching for a word. Hence
it seems justified to count them as (co-)signals of elicitation.
Self-repairs and *turn interruptions* of course also occur in normal
spoken interaction; whether they will call forth a response from
the interlocutor will depend on the extent to which he perceives
the utterance as unsuccessful. *Metalinguistic question intonation*,
while obviously constituting an appeal to the interlocutor, may or
may not by itself work as elicitation. Such intonations on lexical
items are sometimes found in the learner's utterances even where
no WEUs arise.

A closer look at the learner's *elicitation strings* in the pre-
reception phase shows that they tend to be structured in certain
ways. Elicitation strings usually consist of *language switches* and/
or *word construction attempts* as their major components. The use
of switches into English or German (or, occasionally, French) is
obviously conditioned by the fact that SW at the time knew that
these languages were mutually available to both speakers. Switches
used for word elicitations are of a type that we defined in Chapter
2 above as INSERTS, for instance *'feeling'* in example (5). They may
occur either within a FRAME, i.e. an explicit question such as *what's*
in example (5), or just with a metalinguistic question intonation.
Switching can be characterised as a convenient shortcut strategy,
since a switch requires little processing effort and defines the
intended notion very explicitly in terms of a familiar background
language; a switch is, as it were, the lazy way and the efficient clari-
fier. By contrast, attempts at target word construction represent the
more ambitious way in that the learner offers her own suggestions
for a solution to the formulation problem. This often leaves traces
of the processing effort and may form evidence of the current state
of the interlanguage.

In many cases switches and constructions are combined in the
same elicitation string. Then switching may occur either before or
after the corresponding constructions. That is, either the intended
notion is established by means of a switch, as a point of departure,
and is followed by one or more attempts to construct the form,
as for example in (2). Or a form is first attempted and the switch
is added as a cue to the interlocutor, for example in (7). Possible
motivations for a switch in this position are that the speaker is not

satisfied with her construction, that she feels that the intended notion ought to be further clarified, and/or that she feels that a stronger elicitation signal is needed for the interlocutor to react.

(7) S i den = tret- trette / <whats 'third'? = 'third'?>
     B 'den **tredje**'.
     'S in the = tret- trette / <whats 'third'? = 'third'?>
     B 'the third'.'   [0;3.08]

A related type is when the learner resorts to a switch in the following turn as an explanation because the target language speaker fails to understand the construction attempt, as in (8).

(8) S . . . i was going to say> / ja ville säja att han % han **överlignar** = han **överlignar sej**. = % /
     B de förstår ja inte.
     S <**über**' / er '**überlegt** es (B: JAHA) sich'.>
     'S . . . I was going to say> / I wanted to say that he % he överlignar = he överlignar sej. = % /
     B that I don't understand.
     S <'over' / 'he thinks it (B: OH YES) over'>'
     [Target word: *fundera (på det)* 'think (it) over']   [0;1.11]

The construction part often contains a self-repair sequence. Two types of such self-initiated self-repairs occur regularly: a gradual buildup from an initial part to a complete word form, as in (2), (3) or (7), and a string in which the learner works her way from a more L1/L2-based form towards a more purely L3-based construction, as in (9):

(9) S ja är mycke lat. (B: MHM) % därför att ja har % ja har inte gjört gjört en % **ans- ansträngung**¿ / **ansträning**¿ /
     B ja. '**ansträngning**'.
     S '**ansträngning**'.
     'S I am very lazy. (B: MHM) % because I have % I haven't made made an % ans- ansträngung¿ / ansträning¿ /
     B yes. 'effort'.
     S 'effort'.'
     [German *Anstrengung* = '*effort*']   [0;1.11]

It should also be noted that a deictic indication, as in (4) above, is very rarely used by SW as an elicitation strategy; in fact, this is the only example found in the corpus. Switches and construction attempts are the methods she regularly uses to indicate what she refers to.

The *reception point* is the point where the interlocutor supplies or confirms the target word. This is mostly achieved by a simple response turn, but there may also be a negotiating exchange to establish the target word, as exemplified in (3) and (8). The interlocutor may be caused to give or confirm the target more than once, as in (3) and (10), in which case we will count the first instance as the reception point. Defined in this way, the reception point forms the boundary between the learner's elicitation activity (in the pre-reception phase) and securing activity (in the post-reception phase).

(10)	S	å sen % ska ja % t- tälten¿ /	'S	and then % I will % t- tälten¿ /
	B	% 'du ska tälta'.	B	% 'you will camp'.
	S	'tälta'.	S	'camp'.
	B	{ja.}	B	{yes.}
	S	{<thats} 'camping' is it?>	S	{<thats} 'camping' is it?>
	B	ja.	B	yes.
	S	{ja.}	S	{yes.}
	B	{du} ska sova i tält.	B	{you} will sleep in a tent.
	S	ja.	S	yes.
	B	ja.	B	yes.
	S	ja {ska tälta} /	S	I {will camp} /
	B	{de e 'att} tälta'.	B	{that is 'att} tälta'. ['to camp']
	S	ja ska tälta en vecka med en	S	I will camp for a week with a
		% med en bra vän av mej¿.		% with a good friend of mine¿.'
	[0;9.28]			

In the *post-reception phase*, the learner may acknowledge the reception of the target word, request some clarification and/or take steps to secure retention. This will be done by various means, as seen in the examples above:

– a 'yes' answer;
– a citing repetition (metalinguistic citing of expressions is marked

by simple quotes in the transcripts);
- call for confirmation;
- questions about the target word (for example in (10)): its meaning, appropriate use, syntax, or form;
- using the word functionally in a meaningful context (as distinct from a citing repetition);
- re-using the word later in the same conversation.

In the majority of instances, SW confirms reception of the target word immediately by a citing repetition. She usually catches the target form correctly when it is given and very rarely asks about its form, usage or grammatical properties. Post-reception patterns vary from a mere citing repetition to a more elaborate sequence, for example citing repetition – functional use – prompt re-use. It is also rather common for her to go directly from reception to functional use of the word in context, as illustrated in (5) above.

If we consider the overall structure of SW's WEUs and the way they are integrated into the conversational context, the systematic combination of communicative and acquisitional efforts is noteworthy. The WEU always arises in a communicative context and commences when SW calls attention to the intended target word, thus shifting from the level of the conversational topic to the metalinguistic level of word elicitation. The communicative activity then for a while focuses on the word search. But she always resumes her previous thread of discourse after receiving the target word, continuing where the WEU began.

It is obvious that SW in these recordings represents an active type of word eliciter. This is reflected in the high frequency of WEUs in the corpus, in the purposeful way in which she proceeds, and in the range of various strategies that she applies. Presumably this activity level is due both to individual factors (such as her background as a linguist, her language-learning motivation, and a general ease to communicate) and to the type of conversational setting in which a permissive attitude prevailed towards frequent appeal for linguistic items.

4.4 THE ROLES OF THE LANGUAGES

As we can see in the examples given, the learner's background languages are frequently involved in the elicitation attempts, partly in language switches and partly in tentative word constructions. As shown in Chapter 2, there is a strong tendency towards a specific role distribution between the learner's L1 and L2 here. It is primarily L2 (German) which influences word construction attempts and also occurs in automatic, non-intentional switches during formulation in L3. We have referred to this role of supplying language material for the attempted utterances in L3 as a *supplier role*. On the other hand, L1 (English) is the language which most frequently occurs in other types of language switches, which can be associated with various pragmatic functions in the discourse such as editing, commenting, eliciting or clarifying. This role was referred to as an *instrumental role*. To choose one example for illustration, consider again the elicitation string in (2) above, repeated here as (11):

(11)   S   % ja ja va % mycke '<surp- surprised>' / '<über->' / öv-
        över- överräscht / över- överraschade.

The switch *surprised* here is interpreted as an INSERT, used as an eliciting strategy, whereas *über-* is interpreted as a WIPP switch, that is a seemingly non-intentional slip in the production of the tentative L3 forms *överräscht, överraschade*. The target word is *överraskad* 'surprised', and the German counterpart is *überrascht*. Thus the L3 word construction attempt appears to be guided by an equivalent German lexeme, which means that the L2 is also activated in the learner's L3 production.

4.5 LONG-TERM ACQUISITION?

Does the learner retain the elicited words? That is, do the WEUs constitute crucial moments where new vocabulary is durably acquired?

This issue is rather complicated. The long-term retention or non-retention of a new word in the learner's lexicon can be due to many factors. It is difficult to judge the contribution of a WEU in this respect, even on the basis of a longitudinal corpus, not least due to the fact that we cannot control the learner's language use between recording sessions. But still, a longitudinal follow-up of the elicited words in the corpus is not without value, since it may provide some indications. Table 4.1 gives a quantitative overview of the target words and their reappearance patterns.

As can be seen in the table, the great majority of the target words (246 out of 301) were elicited just once; forty-four words were elicited a second time, and eleven words three or more times. The 134 nonce items tell us nothing about retention, but those words which were elicited again or otherwise reoccurred allow some observations. To obtain a schematic comparison, we may contrast the set of ninety words which were elicited once and were then handled correctly (indicating successful acquisition) with the set of words which had to be elicited twice or more (a total of fifty-five words, representing less successful acquisition the first time).

It seems relevant to examine how the learner handles the new item upon receiving it. Bartning (1992), reviewing Py's notion of

Table 4.1   Re-use and re-elicitation of elicited target words

No. of WEUs on same target	Target words	WEUs	Longitudinal pattern			
			Nonce	–R	*R	R
1	246	246	134		22	90
2	44	88		15	5	24
3	7	21		2		5
4	2	8		1	1	
5	1	5			1	
6	1	6				1
Total	301	374	134	18	29	120

KEY:

Nonce = target words elicited once and not reappearing in later recordings.

  –R = target words elicited more than once and not reappearing in later recordings after the last WEU.

  *R = elicited target words which are incorrect at least some of the time when reappearing after the last WEU.

  R = elicited target words which are correct whenever reappearing after the last WEU.

potentially acquisitional sequences, suggests that the likelihood of durable acquisition depends on (a) the more or less explicit manner in which the learner acknowledges the reception of the expression when it has been given, and (b) whether the target expression is re-used in an adequate way later.

To some extent, this can be attested in our longitudinal corpus. SW generally responds in some way to the reception of an elicited lexeme. One may expect that if she uses the elicited word functionally in a communicative context upon reception, rather than producing just a citing repetition or a 'yes' response, this will facilitate retention. A check through the two sets of reappearing target words, inspecting the only WEU in the 'once-and-correct' set and the first WEU in the 're-elicited' set, reveals some quantitative differences. It turns out that such communicative use of the word in close connection with the reception occurs with seventy-four targets (82 per cent) in the 'once-and-correct' set, compared to thirty-seven targets (67 per cent) in the 're-elicited' set. A stronger difference in the same direction appears when we consider whether the learner re-uses the new word in an adequate shape later in the same conversation. This happens in twenty-four cases (27 per cent) in the 'once-and-correct' set, compared to two cases (3.6 per cent) in the 're-elicited' set. This lends credibility to the hypothesis that the communicative and adequate use of the word soon after reception has an effect on long-term retention.

4.6 CONCLUSION

The examples given here show that the learner's attempts to acquire new words during the conversations are systematically structured and form characteristic, regular patterns. We have analysed the learner's behaviour in terms of eliciting activity in the pre-reception phase and securing activity in the post-reception phase. In the case explored here, the learner's driving role in the process is reflected in the intense and varied use of different acquisitional strategies and the high frequency of WEUs in the corpus. We have touched upon the systematic and differential involvement of the learner's background languages in the process. And, distinguishing the notions of short-term and long-term acquisition, we adressed briefly the question to what extent the learner's acquisitional attempts in the communicative situations have a lasting effect on the development of the interlanguage.

Even if WEUs keep occurring in every session throughout the twenty-one-month longitudinal corpus, they are, not unexpectedly, most frequent during the early stage. Thus the majority of the WEUs occur within a couple of months from the start, and most of the examples cited here are from this early period. It may therefore seem tempting to regard word eliciting as a phenomenon specific to language learners, especially beginning and intermediate learners, and to view the use of eliciting and securing strategies as something learner-specific. This may certainly be justified as far as the frequent use of such strategies is concerned. But a look at the various types illustrated above makes it obvious that these types of features can all be recognised in some form in the speech of mother-tongue speakers. These speakers, too, sometimes encounter lexical gaps and need to learn words and appeal to interlocutors. Pauses, pause fillers, iterations, gradual buildups, self-repairs and unfinished turns are of course well known features of ordinary formulation work in conversations, and they may well reflect word search. Appeals to the interlocutor for feedback on formulations also occur among mother-tongue speakers, and means such as metalinguistic question intonation, deictic indications and explicit questions for words do occur. Language switches in interaction between speakers with a native or native-like competence would seem appropriate and natural in settings where the speakers have adopted what Grosjean (1995) has termed a 'bilingual mode', and there seems to be no reason why switches could not be used in connection with appeals for words here. Nor is post-reception behaviour such as citing repetition, checkbacks and purposeful re-use of new words alien to native speakers. Hence what our learner does is to exploit standard verbal means which are available to her as an ordinary human talker, but to an extent which is conditioned by the circumstances. If we thus distinguish the means from the extent to which they are exploited, different learners can be characterised with respect to how variables such as background knowledge and attitudes, perceived needs, learning stage, communicative setting, and so on, influence the extent to which they utilise common human conversational means.

CHAPTER 5

Activation of L1 and L2 during production in L3: A comparison of two case studies

Björn Hammarberg

5.1 INTRODUCTION

The research in recent years on language acquisition by multilinguals has clearly shown that not only the first language, but also languages acquired after the first tend to become activated when the learner attempts to learn an additional language. Studies reported so far with different combinations of languages and different types of learners display a variation as to the extent and ways in which learners draw on previously acquired languages – L1 and L2 – when performing in a new language. These prior languages will here be subsumed under the term *background languages*. A great deal of the discussion has come to concern the various factors which condition the activation of different background languages, and the question which languages are apt to get involved in the use of the current target language. (For an overview of these issues, see for example the contributions in Cenoz, Hufeisen and Jessner 2001.)

In the earlier study reported in Chapter 2 above, the roles which the respective background languages play in the acquisition and use of a third language were investigated. That case study was carried out by Sarah Williams (SW) and the present writer (BH) and was based on longitudinal data from SW's spoken performance as an adult L3 learner. Among other things, it showed a clear division between the roles of the first and the second language, which could be related to SW's linguistic background and the acquisitional setting. These findings received further support in subsequent studies of her pronunciation and her word search during conversation (Chapters 3 and 4). In the present chapter, those prior studies will be taken as a point of departure and data from another adult learner with a partly different background will be presented. The findings from these case studies will be compared and discussed in order to shed further light upon the conditions for the activation of L1 and L2 in L3 production. A third language (L3), then, is defined as a language which is acquired or used in a situation where the person already has knowledge of one or more second languages (L2) besides one or more first languages (L1).

The earlier studies explored, among other things, the learner's use of *language switches* from L3 to a background language (Chapter 2) and her *word constructions* in L3, i.e. her attempts to construct hypothetical words during conversation in L3 under influence from a background language (Chapter 4). The results from these investigations yielded evidence for the roles of the activated background languages in the learner's speech production. A distinction was proposed between two fundamentally different types of roles. A language which is active in the process of communicating in L3 can have an *instrumental role*, to manage the communicative situation, make comments, ask questions, clarify, translate and so on, or a *supplier role*, i.e. to furnish linguistic material for the speech production in L3. Here, our multilingual informant tended to activate different background languages in different roles. The principal supplier language was of course L3 itself (*internal supplier language*), but the project has focused on cases in which a background language, L1 or L2, occurred in the supplier role (*external supplier language*). One notable thing was that our multilingual informant tended to prefer *one* of her background languages in the supplier role: her strongest L2 occurred in her case as *(external) default supplier language*.

In the following, we shall come back to the question of activation of languages and discuss the factors which are found to govern the activation of the various background languages in L3 learners. First, however, the new informant will be introduced, and observations of his language switches and lexical transfer will be compared with the results obtained earlier from the learner SW.

5.2 THE INFORMANTS AND THE DATABASE

The new informant, who we shall call by the (fictitious) initials EE, shows both similarities and differences compared to the learner SW. He is male, with German and English as principal background languages, and started acquiring Swedish at the age of twenty-eight. Conversations with him were drawn from the *ASU Corpus*, a Swedish longitudinal learner corpus compiled at Stockholm University. (Hammarberg 1999 describes this corpus in detail.)

EE was born in Austria with Austrian, German-speaking parents. Due to his father's work on international commissions, he was to spend his childhood and adolescence in English-language environments in various countries, such as Sri Lanka, India, Kenya and Canada, and went to English and American schools. He visited Austria on vacations during his school years, and subsequently spent five years there with university studies, interspersed with periods in Kenya. He spoke German with his parents, but during the years when he was growing up, he used English outside the home, at school, and also with his siblings. In Kenya, he acquired Swahili informally up to what he estimates as an intermediary level. He went to Sweden in order to study medicine and to live with his Swedish girlfriend. In the beginning, he had to take a two-semester preparatory course in Swedish for foreign students. He had spent two months in Sweden before the start of the course, but had mostly used English during this time. He was placed in a class for beginners in Swedish and, after the two semesters, passed the test for admission to regular university studies.

The oral data that were collected from EE consist of recurrent, semi-structured but relatively informal conversations in Swedish between him and two native Swedes. They started at the same time as the preparatory course, but separately from it. They took place on nine occasions distributed over two semesters, plus a tenth occasion as follow-up in the fourth semester. Table 5.1 shows the detailed longitudinal distribution of the recordings with EE. The conversations were audio-recorded and transcribed. They comprise several different activities: interviews, discussions, narrations based on cartoons, as well as descriptions of photos and objects. EE's part of the dialogue comprises circa 18,500 word tokens.

Table 5.1   Longitudinal distribution of recordings with EE

The time-scale is counted from the start of the Swedish course on 27 August 1990, when EE's intensive contact with Swedish began. However, he had then had limited exposure to Swedish in Sweden for circa two months, during which time he spoke mainly English.

Recording no.	Time from start
1	0;2.02
2	0;2.22
3	0;3.13
4	0;4.04
5	0;4.24
6	0;7.07
7	0;8.14
8	0;9.26
9	0;10.17
10	1;9.27

In brief summary, EE's multilingualism can be described as follows:

L1   German (from infancy onwards)
L2   English (at least since school start, native-like level)
        Swahili (intermediary level)
L3   Swedish (observed from beginner level to a fairly advanced level; lived in a Swedish language environment)

Recalling information about SW given earlier (Chapters 1 and 2), she was born and raised in England by English parents. She had studied French and German at university in England and taken a four-week course in Italian in Italy. She then spent six years in Germany, completing a PhD on matters of infant bilingualism, and developing her German to an almost native-like level. At the age of twenty-eight she moved to Sweden for a university teaching job and started acquiring Swedish by practical everyday interaction. Meanwhile, she still had opportunities to use English and German. Her multilingualism can thus be summarised as follows:

L1   English (in current use)
L2   German (near-native level, in current use)
        French (advanced level, not currently in use)

Italian (elementary level, not currently in use)
L3   Swedish (observed from beginner level to an advanced
level; lived in a Swedish language environment)

In the corpus of recorded conversations with SW, her part of the dialogue amounts to circa 37,000 words. As we can see, EE's and SW's multilingualism are similar on several major points, but also differ in some important respects. Both were academically educated and began learning Swedish at the same age, twenty-eight years. Both advanced rapidly in Swedish and used the language actively in communication. The dominating background languages were in both cases English and German, but in different order. EE had attained a native or native-like level in both these languages, even if their functional distribution over linguistic domains was probably not quite identical. Since German was EE's language during early childhood, it should be identified as L1, and English as L2. An important difference between EE and SW is that EE was introduced to a bilingual language environment already as a child.

5.3 ACTIVATION OF BACKGROUND LANGUAGES: LANGUAGE SWITCHING AND TRANSFER

The task of trying to carry on conversations in a new language naturally faced both SW and EE with considerable difficulty, particularly during the first months. This gave rise to various ways for the learner to activate background languages during the conversation in L3. In the analysis of SW's data we distinguished between *non-adapted language switches* and cases of *transfer from background languages in word constructions in L3* (Chapters 2 and 4). Non-adapted language switches were defined as such expressions in other languages, usually a word or a short sentence, as were not adapted phonologically or morphologically to the target language. Expressions which showed traces of being formed under the influence of a background language but were phonologically and/or morphologically adjusted to the target language were interpreted as cases of transfer. It turned out to be important to make this distinction, as these types of activation of background languages tended to involve different languages in our informant and provided an insight into the process of speech production in a multilingual speaker.

5.3.1 Language switching

In Chapter 2, seven different types of language switching were identified, depending on what function they seemed to have in the dialogue. They are illustrated here with examples from EE. (For a key to the transcription, see Appendix 1 at the end of the book.)

(1) EDIT
     (Beginner stage; the learner gets stuck in a formulation:)
     % % å hon / % sen hon fru % och % och och och / % hon fru % % / nej. <na>.
     hon fru % % / dom var % % = % / ja dom var % / nej.
     '% % and then she / then she wife % and % and and and / % she wife % % / no.
     <well!>. she wife % % / they were % % = % / well they were % / no.
     [0;3.13]

(2) META COMMENT
     dom var inte så % dom var inte så roligt % % % / **<i'm losing my vocabulary. i don't know where it is today.>**
     'they didn't have so % they didn't have so much fun % % % / <i'm losing my vocabulary. i don't know where it is today.>'
     [0;3.13]

(3) META FRAME
     % % de var % de var = / **<oh what's the word?>** / <nicht protzig>. ja.
     'it was = / <oh what's the word?> / <not bragging>. yes.'
     (0;2.22)

(4) INSERT EXPLICIT ELICIT
     % % de var % de var = / <oh what's the word?> / **<nicht protzig>**. ja.

'*it was = / <oh what's the word?> / <not bragging>. yes.*'
(0;2.22)

(5)   INSERT IMPLICIT ELICIT
man ser inte så ofta så saker som en j- judiska s- % **<stern¿>**.
'*you don't so often see things like a j- jewish s- % <star¿>.*'
[0;8.14]

(6)   INSERT NON-ELICIT
men dom ha- dom har ingen **<wille>** % som lever längre.
'*but they don't have any <will> % to live longer.*'
[0;7.07]

(7)   WIPP
men de e svårt. för nu e också / **<because>** / för när man bor i
kenya då är mycket swahili också.
'*but it's difficult. because now [it] is also / <because> / because
when you live in kenya then [it]is much swahili also.*'
[0;10.17]

The category EDIT comprises switches which are used to introduce a self-repair, and also interactive feedback signals such as
yeah, okay. The META group comprises metalinguistic elements
of two types: META COMMENT which consists in comments on the
communicative situation or the text itself, and META FRAME which
refers to the frame, usually a question, which sometimes accompa-
nies the words or other expressions asked for by the learner. The
INSERT categories comprise elements which belong to the primary
contents of the conversation, i.e. not editing or metalinguistic elements, and are produced in another language than L3. They are
categorised as EXPLICIT ELICIT if they are accompanied by a META
FRAME, and IMPLICIT ELICIT if they lack a frame but are pronounced
with a rising intonation (which we interpret as an elicitation signal,
'How do you say this?', 'Is this correct?'). In both these cases, then,
we interpret the switch as an attempt to elicit the Swedish expression from the interlocutor. If an INSERT occurs without a frame or
a questioning intonation, it is categorised as NON-ELICIT. Included
here are common cases of non-eliciting switches which may be conditioned by various factors such as lexical gaps, temporary blocking

of access, the nature of the topic or context, the participants' attitudes, and so on.

The last category, WIPP ('Without Identified Pragmatic Purpose'), is of special interest. Whereas all the six previous categories can be related to a pragmatic purpose of some kind in the dialogue, that is not the case here. It seems obvious that whereas the first six types are 'genuine' language switches which do not represent any attempt by the learner to speak in L3, the WIPPs appear just while the speaker is attempting a formulation in L3. The switch itself does not seem to have any function of its own. The WIPP elements are short and most often consist of grammatical function words such as pronouns, prepositions, connective adverbs and conjunctions, rather than content words. A direct self-repair by the learner, or occurrence earlier in the longitudinal corpus showing that these words are known to the learner, will categorise these switches as WIPPS.

If we consider to which languages the switches go, certain differences appear between the categories. Table 5.2 shows the frequency of each category and the distribution of the categories over languages.

It can be seen that EE's switches involve English for the

Table 5.2   Distribution of EE's language switches across functional types and languages

Percentages refer to distribution across languages

Functional type	Switch into						Total
	L1 German		L2 English		Ambiguous Ge/Eng		
	N	%	N	%	N	%	N
EDIT	1	33	2	67	–	–	3
META COMMENT	–	–	6	100	–	–	6
META FRAME	–	–	4	100	–	–	4
INSERT EXPLICIT ELICIT	3	19	13	81	–	–	16
INSERT IMPLICIT ELICIT	7	44	9	56	–	–	16
INSERT NON–ELICIT	31	39	46	58	2	3	79
WIPP	10	13	68	85	2	3	80
Total	52	25	148	73	4	2	204

most part (73 per cent of all instances), and also to some extent German (25 per cent). Switches into Swahili do not occur. This is natural, considering that EE knew that both interlocutors mastered English and German, but that he could not count upon their understanding Swahili. This provided a communicative basis for switches into English and German, but not into Swahili. However, the English dominance varies in strength for different categories. The META switches always go towards English, but the English dominance is also strong for the category INSERT EXPLICIT ELICIT. These are also the cases in which the learner marks most explicitly that he turns to another language than L3. The other INSERT switches are more evenly distributed over languages. The WIPP category, finally, shows a strong English dominance (85 per cent clear instances).

We may compare this to the corresponding data for SW, which are given in Table 5.3. Here, too, the switches are mainly into English and German; switches into French and Italian occur only occasionally. With SW as with EE, the six first categories, i.e. the 'pragmatic' switches, are primarily towards English, and here English also dominates most strongly in the META and INSERT EXPLICIT ELICIT categories. On the other hand, SW's WIPP switches overwhelmingly (92 per cent) occur towards German.

The switching patterns of EE and SW can be summarised as

Table 5.3   Distribution of SW's language switches across functional types and languages

Percentages refer to distribution across languages

Functional type	Switch into			Total
	L1 English	L2 German	L2 French/Italian	
	%	%	%	N
EDIT	70	29	1	82
META COMMENT	100	0	0	73
META FRAME	100	0	0	92
INSERT EXPLICIT ELICIT	89	11	0	150
INSERT IMPLICIT ELICIT	73	24	3	103
INSERT NON–ELICIT	68	29	3	273
WIPP	4	92	4	71
Total				844

Table 5.4   Distribution of EE's switches into GERMAN across types of linguistic units

Functional type	Content words	Function words	Word sequences	Total
EDIT	–	1	–	1
META COMMENT	–	–	–	–
META FRAME	–	–	–	–
INSERT EXPLICIT ELICIT	3	–	–	3
INSERT IMPLICIT ELICIT	6	–	1	7
INSERT NON–ELICIT	26	3	2	31
WIPP	3	6	1	10
Total	38	10	4	52

Table 5.5   Distribution of EE's switches into ENGLISH across types of linguistic units

Functional type	Content words	Function words	Word sequences	Total
EDIT	–	2	–	2
META COMMENT	–	1	5	6
META FRAME	–	–	4	4
INSERT EXPLICIT ELICIT	11	1	1	13
INSERT IMPLICIT ELICIT	9	–	–	9
INSERT NON–ELICIT	37	6	3	46
WIPP	9	58	1	68
Total	66	68	14	148

follows: the 'pragmatic' switches, that is the first six categories, are preferably made into English, which is most typically the case in the most explicitly signalled types of switches. Likewise, EE also makes WIPP switches mostly into English, whereas SW, on the contrary, nearly always makes use of her strongest L2, German.

As mentioned above, EE's WIPP switches tend to be short and mostly consist of function words, rather than content words. The same was the case for SW; see Chapter 2. This is evidenced for EE in Tables 5.4 and 5.5 which show how the various types of switches are distributed over types of linguistic units. The outcome is clear: content words dominate strongly in the INSERT categories, and the function words in the WIPP category. The META categories – recall that they comprise comments and questions – always occur here as sequences of more than one word.

5.3.2 Lexical transfer and word search

We shall count as overt lexical transfer such word choices and word forms as appear to be intended as attempts at formulations in L3, but show trace of having been produced under activation of a background language, an external supplier language. (We must here disregard the likely existence of covert transfer, that is cases where an expression has in fact been formulated under the influence of a background language, but the resulting form is such that this cannot be detected.) Observed instances of transfer will here be called *transfer units*. We thus distinguish between those units which we interpret as the learner's intended expressions in L3 and those morphologically and phonologically non-adapted words and sequences which we dealt with in the previous section.

Some examples of EE's lexical transfer units and their likely sources in the background languages are given in (8)–(11). They are roughly divided into content words (8), function words (9), inflectional forms (10) and lexical phrases (11).

	Interlanguage word	*Target word*	*Source word*
(8)	besena	kvast '*broom*'	Ge: *Besen*
	provingar	prov '*exams*'	Ge: *Prüfungen*
	förkrafta	klara av '*be able to deal with*'	Ge: *verkraften*
	slippa	halka '*slip*'	Eng: *slip*
	tim	gång '*time (in order)*'	Eng: *time*
	färgfull	färgstark '*colourful*'	Eng: *colourful*; Sw: *färg* '*colour*'
(9)	(gå) in (restaurang)	(gå) in på (en restaurang) '*(step) into (a restaurant)*'	Ge: *in (ein Restaurant gehen)*
	sina (fru)	hans (fru) '*his (wife)*'	Ge: *seine (Frau)*
	mest (andra)	de flesta (andra) '*most (others)*'	Eng: *most (others)*
	(anklagad) av	(anklagad) för '*(accused) of*'	Eng: *(accused) of*
(10)	personen	personer '*persons*'	Ge: *Personen*
	avständer	avstånd '*distances*'	Ge: *Abstände*; sing. *Abstand*

(11)	(skriver) med handen	(skriver) för hand	Ge: *(schreibt) mit*
		'(writes) by hand'	*der Hand*
	alla min lev	hela mitt liv *'all my life'*	Eng: *all my life*

Table 5.6 displays the distribution of the various types over background languages. It is seen that lexical transfer occurs frequently from both L1 German and L2 English, yet more from L1 German: 55 per cent clear instances, against 34 per cent from English. (The possibility of influence from Swahili is disregarded here; nothing immediately suggests such influence.) The *content words* are the type where transfer is most frequent; they account for 61 per cent of all transfer units, 114 instances. These are word forms which have been produced under semantic and/or formal influence from a corresponding word in a background language. As we saw in the examples under (8), these items can consist of simple or complex (compound and/or derived) word stems to which the background language has supplied material. It is likely that the similar word formation systems in Swedish and German and the larger number of cognates between these languages have contributed to more transfer from German than from English in the construction of content words. Crosslinguistic influence on *inflectional forms* comes only from German. This concerns mainly plural inflection of nouns, where German and Swedish unlike English have complicated systems of declension which differ in their details. The noun stems which occur here are in all cases similar in form between German and Swedish. When the transfer concerns *function words*, the word produced by the learner usually exists in L3, but the choice of another function word in the target language is grammatically or lexically conditioned. For instance, among the examples in (9) there is a grammatical distinction in Swedish between reflexive *sin fru* 'his (own) wife' and non-reflexive *hans fru* 'his (somebody else's) wife', and the Swedish lemma *anklaga* 'accuse' requires the preposition *för*. The learner has in both these cases chosen according to formal similarity with an equivalent expression in a background language. Likewise, the *lexical phrases* that have been observed are similar in form to a corresponding phrase in a background language. But if we consider the usage at large of function words and lexical phrases in the language, it is difficult to see that one of the background languages should be more similar to Swedish than the

Table 5.6   Distribution in EE of different types of lexical transfer units across background languages

Percentages refer to distribution across languages: % = per cent of total per row.

Type of unit	Influence from						Total
	L1 German		L2 English		Ambiguous Ge/Eng		
	N	%	N	%	N	%	N
Content word	62	54	44	39	8	7	114
Function word	17	37	16	35	13	28	46
Inflectional form	17	100	-	-	-	-	17
Lexical phrase	6	60	3	30	1	10	10
Total	102	55	63	34	22	12	187

other. None of the two background languages seems to be generally closer to Swedish with respect to these categories.

Some cases of lexical transfer in the conversations with EE occur during *word search*, i.e. exchanges where the learner elicits words from the interlocutor. In accordance with the study of word search in SW's case, we shall use the term *word elicitation unit (WEU)* for such a passage in the dialogue (cf. Chapter 4). The phenomenon of word search is interesting in the present connection because it provides opportunities to study the interplay between language switching and formulation attempts in L3 when the learner is acting at the limit of his L3 competence. The WEUs have a typical structure which is illustrated in the examples (12)–(15). ('B' and 'E' are the two Swedish interlocutors.)

(12)   EE   vi har en mycke bra % % % mycke bra % % mycke bra %
         vari- / <variety> / varietet¿. nej. (B: MH) nej de e inte en
         ord.
       B   varietet **variation**. % /
       EE   **variation**.
       E   de e en stor **variation**.
       EE   stor **variation** från <charakter> från alla studenter <in> (B: JA)
         vårt klass.
       'EE   we have a very good % % % very good % % very good %
         vari- / <variety> / variety¿. no. (B: MH) no that is not a
         word.

B   *variety variation.*

EE   *variation.*

E   *there is a great variation.*

EE   *great variation of <character> of all students <in>   (BH: YES)*
our class.'
[0;2.22]

(13)   EE   vi har en gammal system % i medicinstudium. % % vi har alla
% provingar¿ provingar¿ / <or> prover / provar /
E   alla prov?
EE   alla prov. förlåt. (E: JA) alla prov är % % munlig.
'EE   *we have an old system in the medical study. we have all*
% tests¿ tests¿ / <or> tests / tests /
E   *all tests?*
EE   *all tests. sorry. all tests are oral.'*
[Ge. *Prüfung* = *'test'*]   [0;4.14]

(14)   EE   och dom gick ner till en back¿.
E   backe? eller en /
EE   <bach>.
E   bäck.
EE   ja bäck. förlåt.
'EE   *and they went down to a brook¿.*
E   *slope? or a /*
EE   *<brook>.*
E   *brook.*
EE   *yes brook. sorry.'*
[Ge. *Bach* = *'brook'. Sw. backe* = *'slope'; bäck* = *'brook'*]
[0;9.26]

(15)   EE   och han kände dom mycket mycket. och dom % % %
f- / hade förtur¿ / nej / för- förtror = /
E   förtroende?
EE   förtroende <in> hon- / i honom / <in> honom.
'EE   *and he knew them very well. and they % % %*
c- / had confidence¿ / no / con- confidence = /
E   *confidence?*
EE   *confidence <in> hi- / in him / <in> him.'*
[Ge. *Vertrauen* = *'confidence'*]   [0;9.26]

The criteria for identifying a WEU are (a) that the learner shows some activity in order to elicit a word (*target word*), and (b) that the interlocutor provides the target word, or at least confirms a word which the learner proposes. The learner's initiative is essential here. Instances where the interlocutor intervenes spontaneously and corrects an incorrect expression have not been counted. In most cases, the learner will confirm the reception of the target word in some way, by a repetition, a 'yes', by immediately using the word in a formulation of his own, and so on. A WEU then typically consists of three phases: (a) a *pre-reception phase* which contains the eliciting elements; (b) the *reception point* where the interlocutor provides or confirms the target word; and, optionally, (c) a *post-reception phase* where the learner more or less actively adopts the new word. Such three-phase sequences in dialogue have also attracted attention elsewhere, for example in Linell's 'initiative–response analysis' (Linell and Gustavsson 1987; Linell 1998: 165), and in learner contexts in analyses of 'potentially acquisitional sequences' (*séquences potentiellement acquisitionnelles*; De Pietro et al. 1989; Py 1990; Vasseur 1990; Bartning 1992; Bozier 2005). See also Chapter 4 for a detailed description of WEUs as occurring with SW.

The part which primarily concerns us here is the pre-reception phase, in particular the sequence that contains signals that the learner is searching a word. We shall call it the *search sequence*; in the examples (12)–(15) it is that part of the learner's first turn which is marked in boldface. Those signals which can be interpreted as eliciting, and which the interlocutor responds to by providing the target word, can be of different kinds: explicit questions or comments as in (12), a metalinguistic questioning intonation (¿) on a word, a sequence of self-repairs, the gradual buildup of a word-form by repetition as in (15), an interruption of the turn clearly caused by the learner lacking a word, and so on. Such signals are often combined and reinforced by pauses (=) and pause-filling sounds (%).

The search sequence often contains language switches or hypothetically constructed words in L3, or both in the same sequence. They provide insights into the ways the learner utilises his background languages in the process of speaking in L3. Most switches in the search sequences consist of words which correspond to the

Table 5.7   EE's search sequences. Number of occurrences of switches and transfer, counted per word elicitation unit

Type	Switch into	Transfer from	Frequency
1	English	English	1
2	English	German	2
3	English	English or German	1
4	English	no transfer	14
5	German	German	1
6	German	no transfer	4
7	English and German	no transfer	3
8	no switch	English	2
9	no switch	German	12
10	no switch	English or German	8
11	no switch	English and German	1
12	no switch	no transfer	15
Total			64

'English and German' means that both languages are involved in different switches or word constructions in the same unit, whereas 'English or German' refers to word constructions where the supplier language cannot be unambiguously determined.

target word in a background language, as *<variety>* in example (12), or *<bach>* in example (14). They identify the concept for which the learner searches an expression. But also other elements from background languages occur, which do not directly correspond to the target word, for instance function words such as *<or>* in example (13). As for the word constructions, they illustrate how the speaker activates his available background languages in trying to create a wordform in L3.

With EE, a total of sixty-four word elicitation units have been observed. In order to find out how the background languages are distributed in word search, we will focus on how switches and transfer-based word constructions occur and are combined in the search sequences. Table 5.7 gives an overview of this.

As can be seen in Table 5.7, a variety of different patterns for search sequences occur, but with a characteristic distribution. By and large, this confirms the earlier results, i.e. that English is the most common language to switch into, whereas German is the most common external supplier language for word constructions. Switches into English (rows 1–4 and 7) occur in twenty-one WEUs, switches into German (rows 5–7) in eight WEUs.

Table 5.8   SW's search sequences. Number of occurrences of switches and transfer, counted per word elicitation unit

The table disregards occasional instances of activation of French or Italian.

Type	Switch into	Transfer from	Frequency
1	English	English	11
2	English	German	34
3	English	English and German	2
4	English	no transfer	117
5	German	German	16
6	German	no transfer	20
7	English and German	English	1
8	English and German	German	4
9	English and German	no transfer	12
10	no switch	English	3
11	no switch	German	69
12	no switch	German or English	2
13	no switch	German and English	2
14	no switch	no transfer	81
Total			374

'English and German' means that both languages are involved in different switches or word constructions in the same unit, whereas 'English or German' refers to word constructions where the supplier language cannot be unambiguously determined.

Transfer from English (rows 1, 8, 11) occurs four times, transfer from German (2, 5, 9, 11) sixteen times; in addition there are nine ambiguous cases (rows 3 and 10). The most frequent cases are those which contain only switching into English (row 4) or only transfer from German (row 9). In some cases, switching and transfer are combined in the same search sequence (rows 1–3 and 5; five cases in total).

These results can be compared with the corresponding data from SW. She was a more active word eliciter than EE, with a total of 374 WEUs which are summarised in Table 5.8. But the variation of patterns and their distribution over languages resembles what we have seen with EE. With SW, too, switching into English and German influence on word constructions are dominant. The most frequent cases involving background languages are the same as for EE: only switching into English (row 4) and only transfer from German (row 11). It is striking that switching into English is often combined with a German-based word construction (row 2), but that the reversed combination, German switch and English-based word construction, does not occur.

5.4 DISCUSSION

Non-adapted language switches and hypothetical word constructions illustrate different ways for the language learner to activate background languages. It is notable that both SW and EE tend to activate *different* background languages in switches and in word constructions. This suggests that activation of the languages works differently at different stages of the speech production process.

De Bot (1992, 2004) has discussed how bi- or multicultural speakers control their choice of language in the process of speaking. De Bot's first version (1992) proposed an extension of Levelt's (1989, 1993) model of the adult monolingual speaker, which he adapted to the situation of a bilingual speaker. The later version (2004) centres on the multilingual speaker and takes more recent psycholinguistic and neurolinguistic research into account. Certainly, our knowledge in this area is still to a large extent incomplete, but since both Levelt's and de Bot's models are based on a careful evaluation of the available psycholinguistic and neurolinguistic research, it seems motivated to relate a discussion of the observations from SW and EE to them.

Levelt (1989, 1993) represents speaking as a process in which the utterances are successively formed in three subsystems: a *conceptualiser*, a *formulator* and an *articulator*; in addition, there is a mechanism for the reception of speech with components for auditory and linguistic decoding, and a self-monitoring function. The conceptualiser has access to stored extralinguistic knowledge about the world, the situation and the current discourse, and converts intended contents into preverbal messages. The lexical entries, the words, are thought to combine two parts: a *lemma* part which contains the word's semantic and syntactic information, and a *form* part which states its possible forms. The formulator contains a *grammatical encoding mechanism* which accesses lemmas from the lexicon and produces a grammatical surface structure, and a *phonological encoding mechanism* which works on the surface structure and the applicable word forms from the lexicon and produces a phonetic plan for the utterance. This is received by the articulator which produces an overt utterance.

In de Bot's (2004) model of the speaking process in the multilingual speaker, it is assumed that the selection of the language in which to speak is made at the conceptual level in accordance with the speaker's communicative intention. From there it is relayed both to a component of lexical concepts and to a particular *language node* which can communicate directly with both the lemma level, the syntactic formulation level and the phonological-phonetical level and monitor and govern the choice of language at these levels. At each of these levels, the elements of the different languages form language-specific subsets, but also display similarities across languages: lemmas from different languages share semantic features, and syntactic procedures as well as the structure of word forms and the phonological structure have similarities which enable activation to spread between languages. The lemmas of the lexicon contain information on which language they belong to, in addition to the semantic information that makes it possible to choose a lemma which corresponds to the intended concept. De Bot argues on the basis of relevant research that the words in the lexicon are stored in such a way that the access is non-selective. This means that the words in the speaker's various languages can be searched in parallel and compete with each other for activation. The speaker's different languages are also thought to be activated as entire subsets, and each language has, at any given point in time, a default level of activation which is conditioned by various factors: level of proficiency, how much the speaker has used it recently, and so on. Languages tend to become deactivated if not used, or if another language is activated. In the case of trilingualism it has been observed that L2 more than L1 tends to influence the use of L3. Why this is so is still rather unclear; de Bot (2004: 27) advances the possible explanation that 'because the first language is used more, it forms a stronger network which can accordingly be deactivated as a whole more easily than the more loosely organised second and third languages'. The tendency to activate or deactivate non-selected languages also depends on whether the speakers adopt a monolingual or a bi/multilingual *language mode* (Grosjean 2001), that is to what extent it is accepted in the speech situation to switch between the languages and to allow another language than the one selected to interfere. Grosjean (2001:

3) defines *language mode* as 'the state of activation of the bilingual's languages and language processing mechanisms, at a given point in time'. The notion of language mode is also extended to apply to persons who use three or more languages; they can then be in a trilingual, quadrilingual etc. mode (Grosjean 2001: 17f).

How can SW's and EE's language switching and lexical transfer be related to the process of speaking in L3? In de Bot's (2004) model, the selection of language is determined, as mentioned above, at the conceptual level and is controlled via the language node, but activation of elements from another language – or of another language as a whole – can also take place at various stages of the speaking process. A premise for the dialogues with SW and EE was that L3 should be the selected language. Non-adapted language switches of the types EDIT, META and INSERT do not constitute attempts to speak in L3, but rather form instances of a temporary change-over to another language locally in the conversational sequence in order to comment, ask questions, identify wanted lemmas, and so on. This assumption is supported by the fact that non-adapted switches behave differently to forms adapted to L3, in particular that they need not involve the same background language.

For the META COMMENT and META FRAME switches, which represent a shift to a metacommunicative level in the dialogue, the language choice is presumably made in the conceptualiser, under the speaker's control.

The various INSERT switches, which usually concern single content words, arise during the search for a suitable lemma. The speaker finds no adequate L3 lemma in the lexicon, which raises the level of activation for a background language. The speaker probably has more or less control even over these switches. At least in cases where the switch is accompanied by some eliciting element, this suggests that it is controlled by the speaker.

Transfer-influenced word constructions in L3 arise when the learner is faced with the task of constructing the form of the lemma, that is at the word-form level. The task here is to create a form corresponding to a given lemma content, which can plausibly pass as a word form in L3. The examples (8)–(10) above illustrate how activated lemmas in a background language provide models for word constructions.

The WIPP switches mainly concern function words which are

in themselves known to the learner in L3 and are often directly followed by self-corrections. This suggests that they arise in an uncontrolled way during the syntactic formulation process because a background language is strongly activated at the same time. Both SW and EE tended to have their two strongest background languages, English and German, active during the conversations, besides Swedish. In Grosjean's terminology, they were then in a *trilingual mode*. Depending on the degree to which each language is activated in the situation, a speaker can be located along a continuum between a purely monolingual and a bilingual (trilingual etc.) mode. For SW and EE, Swedish as the selected language was of course highly activated in the situation, and English and German somewhat less. Observations over time showed that the levels of activation for the respective languages changed with increased proficiency in Swedish. Not unexpectedly, both switching and lexical transfer became less frequent after the first months in favour of purely Swedish-based utterance production. This indicates that, in terms of language modes, the development went in the direction towards a monolingual mode.

The two background languages appeared on each occasion to have a certain default level of activation. The pattern of switching and transfer in SW and EE suggests, however, that this default level is not invariant throughout the stages of the speaking process, but may differ between different stages of the process. The main observed tendencies as regards preferred languages for switching and lexical transfer can be summed up as follows:

	SW	EE
Language switches		
EDIT, META, INSERT	L1 English	L2 English
WIPP	L2 German	L2 English
Lexical transfer	L2 German	L1 German

In analysing SW's data in Chapter 2, we interpreted this distribution as reflecting the difference between an *instrumental role* and a *supplier role* for the activated background language. An instrumental role manifests itself in non-adapted switches of the EDIT, META and INSERT types, where the speaker makes use of the background languages in various functions which complement and support the speech production in L3, whereas a supplier role for the background language arises during the L3 production itself in the form of WIPP switches and transfer in word construction.

With both learners, *English* is that background language which is most readily activated in an *instrumental* role. This is most obvious in the META switches, where it is particularly evident that the speaker momentarily quits the current topic of conversation, and where the switches always occur towards English. The choice of language for instrumental functions can be explained by several interacting factors.

One necessary condition in order for switching into a background language to be meaningful is *mutual access*, that is the speaker can count on the interlocutor understanding this language. That excludes such languages as Italian and Swahili in the present cases, but makes English and German usable. A further condition is that a *bi/trilingual mode* is adopted. For both SW and EE, the situation was such that the learner felt free to do so. Furthermore, the learner's *proficiency in the target language* is a factor: with increased proficiency the need for language switching decreases. As mentioned, switching was most frequent during the first months for both SW and EE, and then gradually decreased.

Why was English preferred as instrumental language, and not German? The *personal identification* is obviously a factor. For SW this points to English, since she had a clear English identity, even if she was also able to express herself easily in German. As for EE, his identity is not so clear-cut. He could in principle have passed as 'German' or 'English' in the Swedish environment. One additional factor is *the status of the language in question as a contact language*. This favours English as being an international *lingua franca*. In particular, English is the generally preferred contact language with non-Scandinavians in Scandinavia, whereas German is less widely understood in these countries. We must also take into account the language choice that has become *established practice* between the persons in question. In the case of both SW and EE, English was the language which was used by the participants outside the project conversations in the initial period, besides Swedish.

Taken together, all these circumstances make it natural for English to be regularly activated in an instrumental role for both SW and EE, regardless of whether it is first or second language.

The question of which language will be activated most easily as *external supplier* language appears more complicated. We saw that both SW and EE showed most influence from German in word constructions (L2 for SW, but L1 for EE). On the other hand, their WIPP switches showed different patterns, with dominance for L2 German in SW's case and L2 English in the case of EE.

Various factors which have been assumed to affect the activation of a particular external supplier language have been discussed in the literature. In Chapter 2 we proposed the interaction of four kinds of factors, (a) the learner's *proficiency* in the background language; (b) *recency*, that is the extent to which the language has been used lately; (c) *typology*, that is the degree of similarity between the background language and L3, as perceived by the learner; and (d) *L2 status*, the language's status of being an L2 for the learner. Other factors have also been suggested, for instance proficiency level in L3 (Bardel and Lindqvist 2006), whether the background language has been acquired in a natural setting (Ringbom 1987: 113), whether the background language has been used actively (Heine 2002), at what age it has been acquired (Cenoz 2001), and the learner's emotional attitude towards activating the background language (Chapter 1 above). Especially the typology factor has been emphasised in the literature. It seems obvious that it has a great part to play in language constellations where one background language is much closer than another to L3 (see, for example, Chandrasekhar 1978; Ringbom 1987, 2007; Vogel 1992; Cenoz 2001, 2003b; Singleton and Ó Laoire 2006). But the relative strength of the various factors for a given learner in a given situation is far from self-evident. For a particular learner, one factor may differentiate the languages strongly or hardly at all, in terms of default activation level, and thereby become more or less decisive. The relative weight of the different factors *per se* remains unclear for the time being.

With SW and EE, the *proficiency factor* was high for English and German, but lower for French and Italian (SW) and Swahili (EE). Both had acquired English and German in a *natural setting* and used them *actively*, and they had kept both these languages in *recent use* in everyday situations at the time of the project dialogues. These factors obviously provided relevant conditions for a general readiness to activate English and German, but do not differentiate between these languages. The factor *proficiency in L3* appears to have played a certain part for the weaker languages with SW; during the first months when her Swedish was very limited and loosely organised, transfer took place sporadically from French and Italian, but later on, when she had advanced in L3, only German and English caused transfer. (For a discussion of the effect of low proficiency in L3 in combination with low proficiency in an L2, see Bardel and Lindqvist 2006.)

The *typology factor* seems to work both generally and locally in the speech production process. In general, the typology factor speaks against influence from French and Italian in SW and Swahili in EE, and for stronger activation of the closer languages English and German, which also turns out to be the case. Both English and German are similar in many respects to Swedish, and their typological distance to Swedish, generally speaking, does not differ radically. It can be maintained that German has more similarities than English to Swedish in some areas of the language, such as the lemmas in the lexicon, the word formation system and the morphophonological form of words; however, this does not hold true for certain other aspects of the language, such as many syntactic constructions, or grammatical function words. For EE it could be seen in Table 5.6 how different types of lexical transfer units are distributed quantitatively across background languages. There seems to be a correlation between frequency and similarity with background languages for the various types. It is notable that German as a source of transfer dominates most strongly over English in the case of inflectional forms and content words, whereas the languages are more equally distributed for function words.

SW and EE differ with regard to lexical transfer and WIPP switches in a way which is not quite easy to explain. Whereas SW tends to activate the same language, L2 German, for lexical transfer and WIPP, different languages dominate with EE, L1 German for lexical transfer and L2 English for WIPP. In Chapter 2 we interpreted SW's pattern as evidence for a decisive effect of the factor *L2 status*. SW showed an overall tendency to favour her strongest L2 as supplier language. This is confirmed by two other salient phenomena which were observed in the earlier studies of SW. One concerns her pronunciation in L3 (see Chapter 3). Listener evaluations of her performance at the initial stage established that she pronounced Swedish with conspicuously German articulatory settings. The other phenomenon consists in influence from L2 German on L1 English (Chapter 2). It turned out that SW in several of her English utterances during the dialogues produced German-influenced formulations based on German lemmas and sentence constructions based on these lemmas. SW herself noted this with surprise when she later listened to these recorded passages. This, too, was something which occurred mainly during the early period. Taken together, these various kinds of evidence – word constructions in L3, WIPP switches, articulatory settings and influence from L2 on L1 – indicate that SW had a general tendency to keep L2 German strongly activated as external supplier language at least during the early conversations. (Articulatory settings and influence on L1 have not been investigated for EE.)

As we have seen, EE displays a different pattern. He makes use of his L1 as the main source of lexical transfer, but uses the same L2 for WIPP as for other types of switches. A possible explanation may be found in the two learners' relation to their first and second languages. SW had been raised as a monolingual speaker and had learnt L2 German at a linguistically mature age, first through formal foreign language study, and later in her natural language environment. Although her German had reached a near-native level, the distinction between L1 status and L2 status was clear for her languages. It is therefore plausible that the L2 status factor should be of significant importance in favouring German as supplier language in her case. SW also showed an attitude towards L1 which reinforced this; she declared on several occasions in the beginning that she did not want to sound English when speaking Swedish. For EE, the situation was different. Even through German was his family language from infancy, he had grown up with both German and English from childhood and had attended school in English. Therefore, the relation between his German and his English is likely to have been more a matter of domains of use than a difference in nature between an L1 and an L2. Hence we should not expect the L2 status factor to have had a very great impact in EE's case. The fact that L1 German dominates as a supplier in word constructions can be seen in this perspective. Here typological similarity seems to have outweighed the effect of L2 status. The fact that EE mostly uses English in WIPP switches would then not depend on the factor L2 status, but rather suggests that English has been established as the default language to use in switches generally, both in an instrumental and a non-instrumental role.

In summary, the comparison of SW and EE has contributed to shed light on the complex of factors which influence the activation of L1 and L2 when a learner communicates in L3. The results support the fundamental distinction that were proposed earlier in the project between an instrumental and a supplier role. They confirm that the activation of instrumental and supplier languages are determined on different grounds and need not involve the same language. Regarding what determines the use of supplier languages, the principal result is that the significance of L2 status appears to vary individually and to be related to the person's language acquisition history, that is early versus late bilingualism. A continuum is conceivable ranging from balanced bilingualism from infancy (two L1s) to a monolingual childhood and adolescence and the acquisition of additional languages in adult age. EE comes close to the former case, and SW to the latter. The conclusion that there is a connection of this kind between the person's type of bilingualism and the significance of L2 status for the activation of a supplier language must be seen as tentative at this stage. However, it should be possible to test it further in investigations of other multilingual learners.

CHAPTER 6

The factor 'perceived crosslinguistic similarity' in third language production: How does it work?

Björn Hammarberg

6.1 INTRODUCTION

A major theme in the present series of case studies of a multilingual language learner has been the involvement of the learner's background languages in her use and acquisition of the current L3. In earlier studies (see Chapters 2 and 5 in particular), a number of interacting factors were discussed which have been found to promote influence from L1 or a prior L2 on the L3 production process. Put in other terms, we are dealing with factors which cause crosslinguistic spreading of activation of linguistic knowledge from a background language (BL) onto the speaking process during formulation in L3. It was argued that the interaction of these factors determines which BL will take on a prominent role as an *external supplier language* for the L3 user (Chapter 2, section 2.8).

These different factors can be grouped according to type of source (cf. Table 6.1). Some have to do with the properties and mutual relations of the languages involved; such *language relation factors* are crosslinguistic similarity between a BL and the L3 and the case of a BL having L2 status, i.e. being a prior L2 for the learner. Others are related to the learner's linguistic experiences; such *experience factors* include the proficiency level in the BL in question, or in the L3, the extent to which the BL has been used recently, whether it has been naturally acquired, and whether it has been used actively

Table 6.1   Overview of factors causing a background language to become activated in a supplier role during production in an L3

Language relation factors
   Similarity to L3
   L2 status
Experience factors
   Proficiency
   Recency of use
   Naturally acquired
   Used actively
Age
Emotional attitudes

in the past. There are also other individual factors connected with particular languages, such as the learner's *age* during acquisition, and *emotional attitudes* towards using a certain language.

The factor most often dealt with in the literature is *crosslinguistic similarity* between a BL and the L3, also referred to as the *'typology'* factor. In the case of a multilingual learner, the various BLs compete, as it were, for influence on the L3 performance process. If a particular BL shows greater similarity than another to the current L3, this may cause a dominant crosslinguistic influence from the former language. For recent treatments of crosslinguistic similarity in L2/L3 acquisition, see Ringbom's (2007) comprehensive overview of this phenomenon, and also De Angelis' (2007) discussion in terms of *language distance*, in which she gives special attention to the multilingual situation.

The present chapter will explore the function of the similarity factor in the L3 speaking process, drawing examples from the corpus of Swedish conversations between Sarah Williams (SW) and Björn Hammarberg (BH). The main focus will be on the learner SW's lexical inventions, that is her attempts to construct hypothetical Swedish words to express what she is trying to communicate, and the role of crosslinguistic similarity for the activation of background languages in this process. This raises questions such as the following:

- How does the learner perceive and evaluate crosslinguistic similarity?
- Does perceived similarity apply to the language as a whole, or to elements of a language?

- What similarities between the languages play a role?
- What are the learner's options and strategies in making use of similarities?
- How is the similarity factor linked to stages in the speaking process?
- What role does crosslinguistic similarity play in creative construction, and what place does this occupy in the speaking process?

It should be noted that we are restricting the scope in one important respect by focusing on *language production*, and not investigating *language reception*. Obviously, the similarity factor works under different conditions in these two cases. The speech managing process runs in opposite directions: 'from intention to articulation' (Levelt 1989) in production, and from audition to comprehension in the case of reception. In reception, linguistic items are encountered in given contexts, and crosslinguistic similarity interacts with other factors to identify and interpret what is heard. The input may contain items which are new to the learner, but recognisable and comprehensible on the basis of crosslinguistic similarities, extra-linguistic knowledge and cues in the context. The basis for comprehension is thus wider than the learner's current interlanguage. In production, the learner has to supply the formulation and is hence much more dependent on actual knowledge of and intuitions about the target language. It is a topic of this chapter to study the scope for making use of crosslinguistic similarity in this latter situation. (For an extensive treatment of the differences between comprehension and production in foreign languages, see Ringbom 2007.)

6.2 ASPECTS OF CROSSLINGUISTIC SIMILARITY

A basic research problem is to determine how crosslinguistic similarities are perceived and evaluated by the L3 learner. As many have pointed out, it is *similarity as perceived by the learner* that is relevant as a cause of crosslinguistic influence. This was clear already to Weinreich (1953) when he defined *interference* on the basis of the bilingual individual's identifications, as in the following definition of interference in phonology: 'phonic interference . . . arises when a bilingual identifies a phoneme of the secondary system with one in the primary system and, in reproducing it, subjects it to the phonetic rules of the primary language' (Weinreich 1953: 14). Perceived similarity is not necessarily the same as the objective similarity between languages that linguists can identify and describe. In now classical papers, Kellerman (1977, 1978, 1983) explored learners' projections of similarities and intuitions about language distance. He introduced the term *psychotypology* to denote 'the learner's *perception of language distance*' (Kellerman 1983: 114; italics in original). The empirical issue is to find out what learners' perceptions are in given situations of language acquisition, and how this affects their evaluation of language distance.

In practice, language distance or closeness has mostly been judged in L2 and L3 research on the basis of objective facts of typological or genetic relatedness. It may be expected that relative closeness in this objective sense may function well as a predictor of the relative amount of crosslinguistic influence in cases where one BL is much closer than another to the L3. If a clear difference in crosslinguistic similarity is easy to discover, learners are likely to be sensitive to this and tend rather to activate the closer language than the more distant one. On the other hand, when the difference in language distance is small or less clear, it is less obvious how learners will perceive and evaluate relative similarity. In the case of our informant SW, for whom English is L1, German her strongest L2 and Swedish her L3, it is not *a priori* evident how she will perceive and make use of similarities between L3 and the background languages. It therefore seems motivated to look more closely at the role of crosslinguistic similarity in a case such as hers, where two main background languages are both rather close to the L3. We have seen in earlier chapters that German dominates strongly as *supplier language* in SW's production in Swedish, and we have argued that the activation of German is favoured in a decisive way by an effect of *L2 status*, i.e. that German like Swedish, but in contrast to English, is a non-native language for SW. Yet we have also proposed that typological similarity to English and German is one factor that will favour influence from these languages in her case (Chapter 2, section 2.8). A close look at the examples that we have presented in the earlier chapters suggests that SW does make use of crosslinguistic similarities, and that she seems to do this in a selective way. The question, then, is how SW perceives and evaluates similarity with English and German in her use of Swedish.

It needs to be clarified what we mean by 'perceived similarity'. When we speak of 'learner's perceptions', using the term in a broad sense, the different conditions in reception and in production must be kept in mind. In reception, the learner can observe elements in the linguistic input and perceive similarities with elements in background languages. Such observations and perceptions are bound to be selective and subjective, depending on various factors having to do with the speech situation, the discourse context, the composition of the learner's multilingual background, the learner's focus of interest, and so on. Still, in making use of BLs to help decode and comprehend the linguistic input, the learner associates from factual observations. In production the situation is different. The item in the target language is not given, but searched. As Ringbom (2007: 24ff) points out, it is more a matter here of *assuming* crosslinguistic similarity. The learner who is ignorant of a word or a structure in L3 cannot know what it may be similar to in a BL, but has to work with assumptions. The learner has to form conceptions about potential crosslinguistic similarity, and make hypotheses about which BL, and which element in a BL, will be a plausible candidate.

Various kinds of grounds for learners' assumptions seem possible. One clue which may guide the learner is the knowledge or assumption that one BL is on the whole more closely related than other BLs to the L3. It is obvious that SW knew that English, German and Swedish are genetically related Germanic languages, and that she realised that more similarities between them could therefore be expected than to her other BLs, French and Italian; this should make it plausible to make use of correspondences with English or German.

It is not unlikely that the L2 status factor may interact with the closeness/distance dimension and make the learner inclined to expect similarities with an L2 rather than an L1. In SW's case, this would lead her to notice or assume similarities with L2 German rather than with L1 English.

As the learner gets exposed to the L3, a source for conceptions about crosslinguistic similarities lies in the developing L3 interlanguage. Here reception and production will interact. What I suggest is that the early discovery of certain salient similarities between the L3 and a BL will form a basis for the learner to postulate crosslinguistic closeness between these two languages. This will motivate further reliance on this BL when the learner needs other items in L3 in the same area of the language, or further reliance on this BL in general. In other words, the learner may extrapolate from specific observations of crosslinguistic similarity. The early period of encounter with a new language is a phase of orientation, a stage of striving to make out how this language is designed and of getting acquainted with its basic elements and typical features. It is presumably a fundamental strategy for learners to extend early observations so as to form wider conceptions about the target language. Perceived crosslinguistic similarity can be an aid in this process. Such conceptions will subsequently be checked against further input and also be tried out through the learner's own production, and thus be updated and revised successively over time. The empirical question here is which features of the language the learner will find salient and evaluate as indicative of wider similarity.

Apart from the aspects mentioned, which are connected with specific language constellations and acquisitional experiences, speakers have intuitions about language structure which may cause L3 learners to favour or disfavour certain expressions in a BL. Such intuitions may manifest themselves in a preference for the typologically unmarked, as research on implicational universals and SLA has shown (cf. Hyltenstam 1987 for an overview). Another approach centres on what Kellerman has called the *reasonable entity principle* (REP):

> The REP says: 'Treat the L2 [L3 in our case] as if it were a reasonable entity (unless you have evidence to the contrary).' That is, in the absence of specific knowledge about the L2, learners will strive to maximalize the systematic, the explicit, and the 'logical' in their IL. Consequently, L1 structures which would serve to work against the assumed reasonableness of the L2 will tend not to be transferred, and those that would bolster it can serve as transfer models. (Kellerman 1983: 122)

An example of such intuitions in the area of phonology from SW's early exposure to Swedish was cited in Chapter 1 above. SW there commented retrospectively on her use of the word form *sjettar* ['ʃɛtar] for Swedish *kastar* 'throws'. She stated that she had adapted the French verb *jeter* and avoided the English *throw*, 'because it's got a *t h* and Swedish just doesn't happen like that'. By typological criteria, the syllable onset [θr] followed by a diphthong is a highly marked structure. An interpretation of SW's statement in terms of Kellerman's REP is that *throw* did not seem phonologically 'reasonable' to her. It was suggested in Chapter 1 that SW from early on had developed conceptions about what would be phonologically possible in Swedish, which created a 'phonological filter' for possible transfer candidates from background languages.

Does perceived similarity apply to the language as a whole, or to elements of a language? There is evidence in research on language production in bilinguals that languages can be activated as whole systems in the speaker's mind (cf. de Bot 2004: 23). As a result of prior use, a language reaches a *default level of activation* which, if it is high enough, will cause this language to be active in the speaking process. Paradis (1981) proposed the *subset hypothesis*, 'according to which bilinguals have two subsets of neural connections, one for each language, within the same cognitive system, namely, the language system' (quoted here from Paradis 1989: 131). Green (1986), in discussing the control of speech in bilinguals, considers the activation both of individual words and of languages, grading the stages of activation of languages in terms of *selected*, *active* and *dormant*. He proposes that lemmas are labelled with a language tag to identify which language they belong to. Green (1993: 265) suggests that lemmas are organised in the bilingual lexicon into semantic fields and are distinguished crosslinguistically by their language tags; word forms are organised in the lexicon according to phonological properties and are also tagged. The suggestion of tagging the lemmas for language is also adopted by Poulisse and Bongaerts (1994) who propose a spreading activation model in which L2 lemmas are selected in the process of speaking on the basis of conceptual information and the appropriate language tag. Activation may spread through associative connections between lemmas which are similar in meaning, and also spread across languages between lemmas which share conceptual information

(Poulisse and Bongaerts 1994: 41). If activation has a tendency to spread between similar items across languages, and if languages tend to be holistically activated and deactivated as subsets of a common cognitive system, then we should expect a similarity effect both with specific language items and with whole languages. This means that learners would perceive crosslinguistic similarity both between items in languages and between languages as such, and that both item and language similarity would have an effect in influencing learner production.

Let us again consider the various grounds proposed above, on which L3 learners may form conceptions about crosslinguistic similarity. These were (a) knowledge or assumptions about overall language relatedness; (b) the L2 status factor; (c) generalisation from observations of specific facts in L3; and (d) intuitions about unmarked or reasonable structure. As we can see, (a) and (b) apply by definition to whole languages, (c) originates at the item level and may become extended to larger areas of the language or to the language as such, whereas (d) derives from universal properties of language and applies to specific phenomena.

6.3 CROSSLINGUISTIC COMPARISONS

There are various areas of similarity and dissimilarity between Swedish, English and German which can be expected to be salient to persons with a background in English and German who come into contact with Swedish. This section draws attention, in brief outline, to some such areas.

Lexicon. There are extensive similarities between Swedish and German in the vocabulary of *content words*, due partly to common Germanic origin and partly to massive word borrowing from German into Swedish in the days of the Hanseatic League and the Reformation. This is apparently the most striking area of Swedish–German similarity. Cognates with the Germanic vocabulary in English are also numerous, yet limited by the large proportion of Latinate (Romance) words in the central vocabulary of English. Present-day loan words from English to Swedish are certainly frequent, but cannot yet match the earlier German influence. All three languages use a repertoire of 'international' Latin/Greek-based words and regular language-specific ways of adapting them. Rich and productive use of compounding and derivation is characteristic of the Germanic stock of content words in Swedish and German; these languages will often use a Germanic compound or derived word where English uses a Latinate word. Semantic differences in vocabulary are also found more often between English and Swedish. Thus, by and large the vocabulary of content words in Swedish has greater similarity to German than to English. However, this does not hold in the same way for *function words*; here German and Swedish counterparts are often not similar in form, nor in semantic extension. As for *formulaic phrases and idioms*, parallels to Swedish can often be found in English and/or in German, with no immediately obvious tendency as to degree of similarity.

Morpho-syntax. Basic syntax is typologically similar to a great extent in the three languages; thus the general design of Swedish sentence structure is usually not very difficult to comprehend for English or German speakers. Nevertheless there are clear differences. Thus, for example, constituent order in German differs in several respects from Swedish, affecting the placement of non-finite verb forms, direct and indirect objects, predicatives, adverbials, and the finite verb of subclauses. Here English and Swedish are more similar, except for the fact that German and Swedish in contrast to English share the Verb-second rule in declarative main clauses. The German inflectional system is a great deal more complex than that of English or Swedish, with elaborate inflections for number, gender, case, strong/weak agreement, person, and so on. This also means that German makes more use of inflections to signal syntactic functions. Several other phenomena could certainly be mentioned, such as English use of progressive and of *do*-support (absent in Swedish and German), and German lack of preposition stranding (used freely in Swedish and English). But without going into further details, we can conclude that in many central areas of grammar, Swedish shows a greater affinity with English than with German.

Phonology/phonetics. In a phonological comparison of the three languages, Swedish is the one that stands out as different in many respects. Swedish phonology displays a range of typologically unusual phenomena, for example a tonal word accent which interacts with stress accent and is distributed on intricate morphophonological grounds; furthermore so-called complementary length, i.e. a combination of opposite vowel and consonant quantity which also interacts with stress and has an impact on sentence rhythm; a rather complex vowel system including two different types of rounding; a complex set of fricatives; and an assimilatory process of consonant retroflection. Pronunciation is generally an area of Swedish which learners from various language backgrounds find strange initially; SW, too, reported that she only gradually got used to the way Swedish sounds. However, one notable area of relative Swedish–German similarity is the system of stress placement in words, where English differs considerably. This applies not least to cognate words of Latin and French origin across the three languages. Thus the stress pattern complements the Swedish–German lexical similarity noted above. At the level of phonetic detail, it is not immediately clear whether British RP or North German (as in SW's case) is closer to Stockholm Swedish; there are significant differences in both cases. In a comparative survey of pronunciation errors in Swedish with speakers of many first languages, including British English and German, Bannert (1990) notes somewhat more error types with English than with German speakers. For a detailed study of German speakers' interlanguage solutions in Swedish phonology, see Hammarberg (1988). Articulatory settings in English, German and Swedish and the way SW handled them were dealt with in Chapter 3 above.

Even a very brief summary of linguistic properties like the one above shows that ranking languages in terms of language distance is problematic, unless many major criteria support each other and make the distances differ radically. (Ranking, for example, Chinese and English in terms of distance to Swedish would be easier; replace English by Arabic, and the ranking will again be difficult.) The scope of comparison is an important aspect here. It is hard to differentiate the distances of English and German to Swedish if the languages are to be compared as whole sets. Rather, there is a profile of closeness and distance that varies between different areas of the languages. This raises the question whether the learner when perceiving crosslinguistic similarities tends to be particularly sensitive to some types of phenomena in the language.

6.4 SW'S WORD SEARCH: THE SEARCH SEQUENCE

In SW's attempts to find formulations in Swedish, the search for *words* plays a prominent role. Most of the items which she tries to elicit from her L3-speaking interlocutor during the conversations are lexical items. These occasions by far outnumber those where she asks about grammatical structures or pronunciation. The awareness of words has been noted as characteristic of people's perception of language (Singleton 1999: 8f) Assuming a Leveltian type of speech production model (which we have discussed in previous chapters, and to which we shall return below), we can see reasons why a speaker should be expected to focus attention on words. Firstly, access to words comes before sentence processing. According to Levelt (1989), the syntactic and phonological processing in the Formulator needs information from the lexicon to work on, in addition to a conceptually structured 'preverbal message' generated by the Conceptualiser. Secondly, words have to be chosen. The lexical processing involves *selection* of concepts and lemmas from a set of alternatives, and therefore tends to face the speaker with problems of search and dilemmas of choice. The speaker thus tends to become consciously aware of the use of words easier than syntax and phonology which (at least for the competent speaker) are usually processed automatically and unconsciously, given the structure of the preverbal message and the lemmas. For SW in the first months of L3 development, lexical gaps limited her utterance formulation more than missing syntactic knowledge.

Hypothetical word constructions are a characteristic feature of SW's word search. She is far from unique in this respect; the phenomenon is well known in learner production and has been explored in multilingual contexts by several researchers. Thus, for example, Dewaele (1998) analyses the crosslinguistic influence on what he terms *lexical inventions* in learner French. Within a large Dublin project, Ridley and Singleton (Ridley and Singleton 1995a, 1995b; Ridley 1997; Singleton 1999) report on several aspects of *lexical innovations* in learner German, examining for example individual variation (certain learners use them much more), strategical versus impulsive innovations, and connections between use of lexical innovations and learning style. In a study of multilingual lexical organisation, Herwig (2001, 2004) examines learners' word search and tentative word productions during a translation task combined with think-aloud protocols.

In Chapter 4 above, we examined the structure of what we called *word elicitation units (WEUs)*, i.e. those passages in the SW–BH dialogues where the learner attempts to elicit words that she needs from her native interlocutor. As we demonstrated there in detail, these units have a systematic structure which can typically be analysed in three parts, (a) a *pre-reception phase* where the learner attempts by various means to elicit a target word, (b) a *reception point* where the interlocutor provides the word, or approves a form suggested by the learner, and, optionally, (c) a *post-reception phase* where the learner acknowledges the reception of the target word and may make various efforts to retain it in memory. We shall concentrate here on those linguistic elements in the pre-reception phase which indicate the word for which the learner searches an expression in the target language. The text string which expresses the learner's word search attempt will be referred to as the *search sequence*.

By focusing on word elicitation units, we choose to study instances where the learner actively searches a word and where the target word is identified in the dialogue. By these criteria we ensure that the switches and constructions we look at have a pragmatic purpose, i.e. that they are strategic, and that the intended meaning is clear.

As shown in Chapter 4, and similarly with the learner EE in Chapter 5, the intended word can be indicated in the search sequence by a switch to a background language, as in example (1), or by an attempt to construct a plausible word form in L3, as in (2), or by a combination of both, as in (3) and (4). We distinguish between the non-adapted use of a word or word sequence from a background language, which we regard as a language switch, and a morphologically and/or phonologically adapted form, which we interpret as an attempt to construct a word in L3 and regard as a transfer item. In this connection we shall leave aside cases where a hypothetical word construction is formed purely on the basis of the learner's current L3 interlanguage, i.e. intra-L3 constructions. In the examples below, the Swedish target word is listed first, followed by its English and German counterparts. Note that text strings interpreted as language switches are put in angle brackets. For a full key to the transcription conventions, see Appendix 1.

(1)   Target: *skruva* E: *screw* G: *schrauben*
       ja tycker att % man måste = / <'to **screw**'?>
       'I think that % one has to = / <'to screw'?>'   [0;6.26]

(2)   Target: *knackar* E: *knocks* G: *klopft*
       när hon **kloppar**¿ klopp- /
       'when she knocks¿ knock-'   [0;0.29]

(3)   Target: *artig, hövlig* E: *polite* G: *höflich*
       ja vännerner+ är kanske lite för % / <whats 'polite'?> 'höfligt'?
       'well, the friends are perhaps a little too % / <whats 'polite'?>
       'höfligt'?'   [1;1.18]

(4)   Target: *yta* E: *surface* G: *Oberfläche* Topic: describing a door hinge
       ja måste tillbringa den på dörren och på en annan överfläck.
       (B: MHM) '<surface>'. (B: MH) 'överfläcken'.
       'I must fix it on the door and on another surface. (BH: MHM)
       '<surface>' (BH: MH) 'the surface'.   [0;7.18]

These examples demonstrate the two principal ways in which SW indicates the word she is searching for. In (1) she resorts to an English lemma for which she requests a Swedish counterpart. In (2) she ventures a hypothetical Swedish word form. The form *kloppar* shows that she has a German lemma in mind, as well as its form, which she tries to adapt to Swedish. There is an additional point in orienting her word construction attempt to a background language to which both speakers have access: this will supposedly make the form transparent to the interlocutor even if it should not be correct, and thus will help clarify which concept she wants to express.

Examples (3) and (4) show two ways of combining a switch and a construction attempt. In (3), SW starts by defining what she intends to say by means of an English lemma, and then offers an attempt to formulate an L3 word. In (4) she first constructs a word form and then confirms by a language switch what it is intended to mean.

The distribution of languages involved in switching and constructions in word search was analysed in Chapter 5 above. Table 5.7, which tabulates the patterns of switching and construction in 374 word elicitation units from SW, demonstrates her strong preference for using English for switches but German as a supplier language in word constructions.

6.5 WORD CONSTRUCTION ATTEMPTS

A closer study of SW's word construction attempts in the search sequences reveals ways in which she evaluates and makes use of potential crosslinguistic similarities. Both English and German offer options for construction attempts, but it can be seen that SW has a preference for certain strategies, as the following examples will show.

Although German influence predominates generally, there are also a number of straightforward instances where English source words are made use of, as in (5):

(5)   Target: *köerna* (*kö+er+na*, Plural Definite) E: *the queues* G: *die Schlangen*
      ja märkade inte % kj- kjuenar¿ / '<the queues>'?
      'I didn't notice % qu- the queues¿ / '<the queues>'?   [1;2.10]

Some further examples are listed in (6):

(6)	*SW's form*	*Target*	*English gloss*	*German gloss*
	briba	muta	bribe	bestechen
	utor	annars	otherwise	sonst
	viska	visp	wisk	Schneebesen
	pluggan	kontakten	the (electric) plug	der Stecker
	hjälpfull	hjälpsam	helpful	hilfreich

Some examples with German source words are shown in (7) and (8):

(7)   Target: *drömmer* E: *dream* G: *träumen*
      dom sitter % i bilen och % tråma¿ / '<dream>'? 'tråma'?
      'they sit % in the car and % dream [= they are sitting in the car dreaming] / '<dream>'? 'dream'?   [0;2.15]

(8)	SW's form	Target	English gloss	German gloss
	alejne	ensam	alone	allein
	ågen	ögon	eyes	Augen
	fifer, fiffer	visslar	whistles	pfeift
	langvilt	tråkig	boring	langweilig
	förglickt	jämfört	compared	verglichen
	tritt	steg	step	Schritt, Tritt
	osten	påsk	Easter	Ostern
	läckelt	lett (Inf: le)	smiled	gelächelt
	tatsak	faktum	fact	Tatsache, Faktum
	perycke, peryck	peruk	wig	Perücke
	hintergrund	bakgrund	background	Hintergrund
	hänger från	beror på	depends on	hängt von . . . ab

Even in cases where the English and German counterparts are cognate to each other and SW's form resembles both, as with *tråma* in (7) and *alejne* in (8), the degree of form similarity reveals that SW in these cases had a German lemma in mind.

It is striking that SW often tends to rely on a German compound or derived lemma using 'Germanic word-formation'. Examples (9) and (10) illustrate this.

(9) Target: *sälja* E: *sell* G: *verkaufen*
skulle jar+ = förkörpa+¿ / <'i would sell'?>   [0;1.05]

(10) Target: *sammanfattning* E: *summary* G: *Zusammenfassung*
en % <summary> <ein> tillsammensfassning.   [0;1.11]

In (9) the complex German word *verkaufen*, derived from *kaufen* 'buy', forms a source of transfer, rather than the simple English word *sell*. Morphological simplicity does not seem to have a significant influence on constructing a plausible lemma.

Example (11) illustrates how SW activates a German separable verb compound and tries to adapt it to Swedish. The first construction attempt reflects the syntactic properties of the German lemma, which affect the word order. In this type of verbs in German, the adverbial element is placed separately after finite verb forms, but prefixed to non-finite forms. The second construction attempt in (11) is a repair in the direction of Swedish structure.

(11)   Target: *föredrar* (Inf: *föredra*) E: *prefers* G: *zieht vor* (Inf: *vorziehen*)
       i sommar % **f- %** / **'<he prefers>'** / % **drag <er> för¿** / **<er>**
       fördrag¿ /
       'this summer he prefers'
       [German: *diesen Sommer zieht er vor*]   [0;1.05]

One theoretically available way of inventing words in L3 would
seem to consist in making systematic use of the 'international'
vocabulary which is current to a greater or lesser extent across
European languages, with language-specific form adjustments.
This could conceivably be used as a regular strategy. But SW
very obviously avoids this in her word search. Instead she tends to
favour Germanic word-formation. Example (12) is an illustration.

(12)   Target: *effekt, verkan* E: *effect* G: *Auswirkung, Effekt*
       ja tycker att de de måste ha en = % en **ut- utvi- -virkn-** / <% whats
       whats % % 'it it must make some kind of' % **- - - <'aus-**
       auswirkung'>.
       'I think that it must have an - - - effect'   [0;3.08]

SW's word search often gives rise to a repair sequence starting
from a German or English source and working its way towards a
supposedly more Swedish form:

(13)   Target: *undervisa, lära ut* E: *teach* G: *lehren*
       ja tycker om % **lären** / **lä- lärare.** ja tycker / **- - - ja** tycker om % **att**
       lärare / **att lära.** **<i like teaching.>**   [0;0.22]

(14)   Target: *strukturerad* E: *structured* G: *strukturiert*
       strukturiert / **struktu- strukturerad¿** (B: MH) **strukturerad**
       [0;5.15]

(15)   Target: *äggklocka* E: *egg timer* G: *Eieruhr*
       de är en % **ägg- = äggtider. - - -** de är de är en % **ägg- % äggväck-**
       / **äggalarm.** de är en (B: JA) **äggalarmaring+.**   [0;6.26]

In (13) and (14) the repair aims at developing a more adequate form
for the lemma that SW has established, whereas in (15) the change
affects the lemma itself.

SW very early tries to inflect the words that she constructs. In most cases, inflections are Swedish-based. But sometimes constructed forms appear with German-based inflection, especially in the first construction attempt in a search sequence. This could be seen in (13) and (14), and the following two examples are further illustrations.

(16) Target: *klasser* E: *classes* G: *Klassen*
      två klassen; / % klassor   [0;0.22]

(17) Target: *tälta* (cf. *tält* 'tent') E: *camp, sleep in tent* G: *zelten*
      å sen % ska ja % t- tälten; /
      'and then I'll camp'   [0;9.28]

English-based inflections on hypothetical word constructions do not occur in the data. This suggests that Swedish, German and English are ranked in a hierarchy of decreasing availability for supplying inflection forms. The form *klassen* in (16) could be German-based as a chunk, but this does not go for *tälten* in (17), where a German-based infinitive suffix is attached to a Swedish stem.

When word constructions in L3 are formed under the influence of a background language, both the L3 and the BL by definition serve as supplier languages; transfer items are thus linguistic hybrid formations. It is conceivable that more than one background language could contribute to an L3 word construction; but this is rarely attested in SW's data. There are some instances, to be sure, where the English and the German equivalent are very similar to each other and both appear to support the learner's form, such as the examples in (18):

(18) *SW's form* *Target*   *English gloss*   *German gloss*
      lärna   lära sig   learn   lernen
      bringa   ta in   bring in   hereinbringen

But clear examples where an L3 form shows traces of two different background languages are practically lacking in the data. (A couple of counterexamples produced in special situations are (19) and (20) below.)

The setting in which SW is carrying on these conversations is such that switching and crosslinguistically based word construction is allowed, i.e. she is acting in a *multilingual mode* (cf. Grosjean 2001). This sometimes leads to complex cases of multiple language activation with crosslinguistic effects on background languages, such as those illustrated in (19), (20) and (21):

(19)   Target: *par* E: *couple* G: *Paar, Ehepaar*
       de finns en = / ja. <whats 'a married pair'? 'married couple'?>
       / de finns en **pär** . . .
       'there is a = / well. <whats 'a married pair'? 'married couple'?>
       / there is a couple . . .'   [1;3.00]

This example was cited in Chapter 2 together with a number of other instances which showed that German was so strongly co-activated in the speech situation that it could even influence SW's English utterances. Here, German *Paar* is activated when SW wants to express 'a married couple', producing *a married pair*. The German-English *pair* then gives rise to the form *pär* in her L3 production.

(20)   Target: *nerför (trappan)* E: *down (the stairs)* G: *(die Treppe) runter*
       han han **springer** % **trappan** % han **springer** <unten+> / <not>
       'han **springer** under **trappan**'. - - - han **springer trappan
       runter+**.
       'he runs down the stairs'   [0;1.11]

Example (20) concerns the syntax of the lemma meaning 'down' and is complicated by the different semantic extension of the corresponding concepts in English and German. Firstly, English *down* is constructed as a preposition, like Swedish *nerför*, whereas German *runter* is postposed. Secondly, *down* can refer either to a direction/movement, as here, or to a position. Only the former applies to *runter*; the German lemma expressing position is *unten*. Swedish *nerför* expresses a direction. This gets tangled up for SW who produces something which appears like 'he runs the stairs – he runs down [Position] – he runs under the stairs – he runs the stairs down [Direction]'.

(21)   Target: *vänlighet* E: *friendliness* G: *Freundlichkeit*
       (Cf. *vänskap/friendship/Freundschaft*)

ja tycker om <die> vänlich- % -skap; / '<die> vänlichheit'
'<friendliness>'.
' *I like the friendliness* '   [0;0.29]

In (21) there is a closer connection than usual between switching
and constructing. The relatedness between the concepts 'friendliness' and 'friendship' also plays a part. The German suffixes -*lich*
and -*heit* occur in the word constructions in L3. An interesting
detail is the -*heit* in *vänlichheit* which, in German, should come
out as -*keit* in the position after -*lich*. SW of course knew this
regularity well and normally mastered it. But it is dropped in the
crosslinguistic formation process, possibly under the influence of
the corresponding Swedish suffix -*het*.

6.6 LEXICAL PRODUCTION IN THE L3 SPEAKING PROCESS

Pursuing the earlier discussions (in Chapters 2 and 5) of the L3
speaking process, we will consider the role of perceived crosslinguistic similarity at the various stages of lexical production during
SW's word search. The discussion will be oriented to de Bot's
(2004) multilingual processing model, which was summarised
briefly in Chapter 5, section 5.4, and to Levelt's (1989, 1993, 1999)
model for the monolingual speaker which underlies de Bot's multilingual model of lexical processing. (De Bot refers particularly to
Levelt's 1993 version.)

In Levelt's model of speech processing, formulation is lexically
driven; it is crucial for the speaker to come up with words, *lemmas*,
on which sentences can be built. In the learner's search for words
in L3, the intended *lexical concepts* are to be realised as lemmas
retrieved from the L3 lexicon.[1] The problem is that the L3 lemma
is often not known by the learner, yet the lexical concept that the
learner has in mind needs to be expressed somehow. As we have
seen, SW displays two different ways of doing this, either by a
language switch or by a word construction attempt.

We have interpreted switches of this kind as the temporary selection of another language in order to make clear what lexical concept
the speaker has in mind, thus not as a formulation attempt in L3.

The processing model of de Bot (2004) locates language choice at the conceptual level of processing; in accordance with that, this is also where these switches should be assumed to take place. Crosslinguistic formal similarity between words plays no part in the switches. However, a lexical switch which is used for eliciting a word hypothesises a semantic correspondence, i.e. assumes that there is a word in the L3 corresponding in meaning to the one in the background language.

Examples of switching which are not accompanied by construction attempts, such as (1) above, illustrate cases where the lexical production stops at the conceptual level (at least for this turn in the dialogue).[2] During the conceptual preparation of the utterance, the speaker generates a concept but does not try to formulate it in the target language. Instead, the intended concept is identified by means of a lemma in a background language. Word constructions, on the other hand, express *lemmas* which the learner tries to establish in L3, as well as their hypothetical *forms* (or *lexemes*).[3] We must conclude that this part of the process takes place in the lexicon.

This brings up an aspect of lexical access which, as far as I am aware, has received little attention in current models of the speaking process, namely the difference between *retrieving* and *constructing* words. In view of what is known about productive means of word formation in languages and lexical innovation in normal speech, the lack of concern with this in the current speaking models seems surprising. However, Levelt (1989: 185f) touches on this problem in discussing the lexicon. The mental lexicon, in Levelt's model, is assumed to be a passive store of declarative knowledge about words. Speakers access lemmas for the grammatical encoding by retrieving them from this store, and subsequently, during the phonological encoding, activate their appropriate forms. But it is obvious that people also regularly generate new words when they speak, which Levelt also points out. This means, he concludes, that speakers must have access to lexical procedural knowledge and a processing component dedicated to lexical encoding, which produces new words as output. Some lexical constructing is likely to occur in all languages. But, according to Levelt, languages vary greatly as to the extent to which new words are generated in the course of speaking. He places English at one extreme of a continuum, stating that English speakers rarely create new words by lexical encoding;

instead, the corresponding purpose in formulation is served by syntactic encoding. At the other end of the scale, he sees such agglutinative languages as Turkish and Finnish, in which very rich means of productive word formation permit frequent construction of new words while speaking. Levelt refrains from a deeper discussion of the process of lexical constructing, on the grounds that too little psychological research on this matter is available. But the fundamental point remains that a complete theory of the speaking process must recognise the existence of a lexical encoding component which enables new words to be constructed in the speech situation.[4]

The possibility of not only retrieving, but also constructing words is a crucial point. For learners this means that they will utilise and extend a faculty which they already possess as native speakers. The sometimes fanciful word creations that children tend to make in their first language are a well known parallel in L1 acquisition. There is, however, one significant difference between mature native speakers and language learners. Whereas native speakers normally create new words in a regular fashion, according to the productive rules of their language, learners at early stages of acquisition may have to work more tentatively, trying to come up with lemmas and forms which are as plausible as possible. The learner who is ignorant of a word may hypothesise a lemma and creatively construct its morphological design and phonological form. When the native speaker has decided on the lemma's conceptual content, syntactic properties and morphological structure, the appropriate form can be accessed in a regular way. But the learner will still have creative work to do at this point.

SW's word constructions point to crosslinguistic influence both at the conceptual and lemma level and at the form level: the examples show that the lemma is regularly taken over from a background language.[5] This should be interpreted as conceptual transfer in the first place: the learner assumes that a concept which is lexicalised in the background language has a direct counterpart in the L3. This leads to transfer at the form level: the BL lemma's word formation structure and phonological form serve as models for the construction of a hypothetical L3 word form. The lack of knowledge in the L3 will raise the activation level of one or more background languages – in SW's case most often German. It also becomes clear that she tends to favour certain lemma-creating strategies, such as activating 'Germanic word-formation' and deactivating 'international words'. Presumably the morphological and phonological structure of a known lemma in the BL plays a part in causing the learner to activate this lemma if there is a choice between alternatives. Here a form-based transfer mechanism appears to be at work. A certain word in a BL may satisfy more general requirements of word-form construction in L3. For example, if the learner has a preference for making use of Germanic word-formation, then she might search for a known word of this type in a BL to use as a model (which will make SW pick a German word most of the time). There may be a sensible reason for a learner in this situation to opt for complex words with a transparent morphological structure, rather than simple words or complex ones of a more opaque structure; a system of productive compounding and derivation allows the speaker to build words ad hoc and may therefore appear useful as a 'construction kit' for tentative word form creations.

There are also a couple of other possible reasons why the learner will attempt a certain word form. One is the possible interaction with the L2 status factor. In the case just mentioned, Germanic word-formation means stronger reliance on L2 German, and the use of international words would mean an orientation to vocabulary that is familiar from L1 English. Another reason could be that the learner has in fact encountered the L3 word before and has some remaining vague memory trace of what it was like, which causes her to attempt a certain construction. In this case, (more or less vaguely) perceived similarity with a BL word may of course be an influencing factor.

Sometimes the learner's word constructions may be related to problems at the conceptual level, as for example in (21). Here the form *vänlichskap* suggests that activation has spread between the concepts 'friendliness' and 'friendship' and that this has been strong enough to cause interference between the two in the word constructing situation in L3. Two lemmas (or fragments of them?) have been activated and become mixed in the output.

Syntactic properties may also cause problems which result from the activation of a BL lemma, as we saw illustrated in examples (11) and (20).

SW regularly tries to adapt the segmental phonological form

of the constructed words to the L3. The transcripts render this in the framework of Swedish spelling. Thus for example, *briba* 'bribe' in (6) is pronounced with an [iː], and not with the English diphthong.

Bound morphemes are often based on Swedish – (9), (10) and (12) are illustrative examples. Here SW obviously has acquired some common Swedish word formation elements such as *till-*, *för-*, *ut-* and *-ning*, and they are used in the word construction.

Inflectional elements are usually supplied by the selected language, Swedish, even where the lemma is modelled on a BL. This is part of the word's adaptation to the L3. It is the same phenomenon that regularly occurs in loan word adaption in native speakers' usage: the stem is borrowed but the recipient language supplies the inflection. What is noteworthy is that SW sometimes takes inflectional elements from L2 German, as illustrated in examples (13), (14), (16) and (17). This L2 here assumes a role which is normally fulfilled by the L3 itself. By contrast, elements from English do not occur in inflections. This underscores the role of German as *default external supplier language* for SW and confirms that German tends to be strongly co-activated in her word construction.

There is apparently an ongoing competition for activation between the selected language and the external supplier during word construction. Evidence for this are repair sequences such as in examples (13)–(16) where SW strives to replace initial construction attempts influenced by the BL by approximations to the L3. At the initial attempt, the lack of an available L3 lemma enhances the activation of a lemma from a BL. However, the result leaves the learner unsatisfied, so she makes a new attempt trying intentionally to deactivate the BL and strengthen the activation of her L3 interlanguage knowledge. Thus self-monitoring and self-repairing of the construction attempts is a part of SW's word elicitation activity.

6.7 CONCLUSION

The findings presented in this and the foregoing chapters show that SW had a strong tendency to activate items and patterns from her prior L2 German in her L3 Swedish production, especially at early stages of L3 acquisition. This was attested in several different areas of the language: WIPP switches (Chapter 2), articulatory settings (Chapter 3) and word constructions (Chapter 4 and the present chapter). Even SW's English utterances were sometimes influenced by German (Chapter 2). These various findings suggest a *default level of activation* for German as a subset of her multilingual competence, which was high enough to make it co-active on a regular basis during SW's utterance production. We have referred to this earlier as a *default supplier* role for German (Chapter 2, section 2.8).

In Chapter 2, we argued that the combined effect of higher proficiency, greater typological proximity and more recent use favoured crosslinguistic influence from English and German rather than French and Italian, whereas the effect of L2 status was considered crucial in favouring German over English in the role of *default supplier*. In the present chapter we have further explored the workings of the typological factor. We may distinguish two aspects of this issue: first, does the typological factor (more precisely, perceived crosslinguistic similarity) have a role in establishing a default supplier role for German rather than English? And second, how is crosslinguistic similarity handled in the process of formulation?

In regard to the first question, it is clear from SW's word construction attempts that she tends to assume far-reaching similarity between the Swedish and German lexicons, especially in the area of content words. Her conception of this surpasses the factual similarity between the two languages and plays down existing similarities with English. I suggest on the basis of the considerations above that this is conditioned by a combination of the learner's pre-established notions of language relatedness and the effect of L2 status for German on the one hand, and the process of generalising early observations of crosslinguistic similarities from the input on the other. Similarities observed in the input apply especially to certain areas of the language, notably content words.[6] By contrast, a phenomenon such as German articulatory settings (Chapter 3) is not likely to depend on factual observations of similarity, especially since they occur in SW's Swedish pronunciation at the very outset. Nor is the dominance of German influence over English on WIPP switches likely to have arisen from observations of cross-language word correspondences, but rather appears to be an effect of high overall activation of German during the formulation process (cf. Chapter 2, section 2.6.4).

As for the second question, we have looked particularly at SW's conceptions of plausible L3 words in situations where she cannot retrieve an L3 lemma, but tries to elicit one from her native L3 interlocutor by offering a hypothetic word form. One observation we have made is that she acts in a selective way, favouring certain options and disregarding others. A way of exploiting crosslinguistic similarities would have been to rely on international, Latinate words which she could expect to find in Swedish as well as in English and German. But she tends to avoid this – (12) is an illustrative example. On the contrary, she shows a preference for complex words of Germanic origin, where she tries to use Germanic word-formation mechanisms to build word-forms. The possibility of constructing tentative words in this way may be a contributory reason for her to fill lexical gaps in L3 with lemmas taken over from German.

A further observation is that creative lexical construction is a more important part of the speaking process than what appears from the minimal attention it has received in current speaking models. The construction of novel words by productive means of word-formation is a natural linguistic resource in native speakers' production, and it may be exploited in a tentative way by learners. In SW's case it is used strategically in acquisition, as a means of eliciting vocabulary during conversation. As we have seen, her attempts are guided by her perceptions of crosslinguistic similarity.

Previous research indicates that there is considerable variation between individual learners in the extent to which they make use of creative word construction (Ridley and Singleton 1995a, b). SW made maximal use of this facility, making it a favourite strategy in word search in the recorded dialogues. Creative word construction can be expected to occur frequently if certain conditions apply to the speech situation and to the learner as a person. Several such conditions were met in SW's case. Thus, a multilingual mode of speaking was spontaneously adopted and accepted in the dialogues that were recorded. SW as a learner was an uninhibited linguistic risktaker; she rather seemed to enjoy trying out possible words in L3, and making errors did not embarrass her. At the same time, her motivation for vocabulary acquisition was strong; she needed it in her new job and living environment. In the turns of the conversation, she was also focused on communicating the current message and the intended concepts, which motivated word elicitation. Finally, there was surely an element of curiosity involved; being a linguist and a multilingual, she was apparently challenged to discover what the language she had taken on was like.

NOTES

1. In de Bot's (2004) model, a *lexical concept* produced at the higher, conceptual level of processing activates a *lemma* in the lexicon by matching their semantic content. In the revised, 1999 version of Levelt's model, the intended semantic information of the word to be produced is contained in the lexical concept, and the lemma, in a narrower definition than in Levelt's earlier model versions, primarily specifies the word's syntax. That is, after conceptual preparation, the preverbal message consists of a conceptual structure containing 'concepts for which there are words in the language' (Levelt 1999: 87). Cf. also Levelt, Roelofs and Meyer (1999) for a comprehensive spreading-activation theory of lexical access in (monolingual) speech production, which presents a model for the conceptual preparation leading to the activation of lexical concepts; in the present connection, see particularly pp. 2 and 37, fn. 1. Here, the authors also argue for abandoning the term *lexeme* for the lemma's *form*, since it tends to cause confusion.

2. In the word elicitation situations under consideration here, the continued dialogue will provide the target word and usually cause the learner to produce an L3 word form in a subsequent turn. But in other, non-eliciting situations (which are not studied in this chapter), the missing word may be replaced by a switch only.

3. See end of note 1.

4. The crosslinguistic variation that Levelt posits for word constructing may have some bearing on SW's multilingual situation. My general impression is that both Swedish and German speakers quite frequently form new words while speaking.

It is possible that they rely on such spontaneous word construction more than English speakers do. Such a practice will draw on productive means of compounding and derivation. Certainly, this possible crosslinguistic difference would need to be substantiated by a controlled investigation of native speakers' actual usage which, however, is beyond the scope of the present study. But if it is true, it means that this could be an aspect of the language where Swedish and German usage show similarity and differ somewhat from English usage.

5. As mentioned above, we here disregard purely intralingual formations, i.e. those based exclusively on material from the learner's current L3 interlanguage.

6. An examination of syntactic structures in SW's production (which has not been undertaken) might reveal further areas of observed similarity.

Appendix 1: Key to transcription

The examples are rendered in the transcription which is used in the source corpora (the *Processes in L3 Acquisition Corpus* in Chapters 1, 2, 3, 4 and 6, and the *ASU Corpus* in Chapter 5). A modified form of standard Swedish orthography is used, in which the common 'spoken language forms' (such as *de, va, mycke* etc. for standard written *det, var, mycket* etc.) are rendered when the speaker uses them. In addition, the following special symbols are used:

=	empty pause
%	pause filler
-	interrupted word
+	morphologically unclear ending
/	interruption, reformulation; non-completed sentence
\	at the beginning of a turn if this is a continuation of the speaker's previous utterance
?	completion of question sentence
.	completion of a sentence other than question
¿	questioned expression (indication by intonation that feedback is required pertaining to this item)
' '	used when the speaker quotes an expression
<>	used around a non-adapted switch into a language other than L3
( )	around capitalised text within speaker's turn: interlocutor's feedback insertions
{ }	overlap: simultaneous speech by two speakers

The time of the recording, counted from the startpoint, is given in square brackets in the form [year;month.day]. Thus, for example, [0;3.13] means that the example was recorded 0 year, 3 months and 13 days after the startpoint. For SW, this point was set to the day of her arrival in Sweden fourteen days prior to the first recording. For EE (Chapter 5), the start of his Swedish language course was taken as startpoint. See Tables 2.5 and 5.1, respectively, for overviews of the time scale.

Appendix 2: SW's narration of the picture story *Hunden* 'The dog'

det är en gammal huset. (B: JA) % en man % e framför huset. % e tid- tidnings- tidningsman (B: MH) % % sj- sjettar la sjet- % sj- sjettar tidning <in den in den garten>. = % hunden % / % de där hunden = hunden % vill ha den = tidning. % hunden == hunden har = tidningen. % / ah. hunden springer / mhm. / ha- / hunden springer framfor = å tar = tidningen. (B: MH) % går % går till huset. % hunden läser tidningen = framf- framför huset. (B: MHM) % de- den gammal / det gammal man röker. ja.

English gloss

There is an old house. (B: YES) A man is in front of the house. Is newspaperman. Throws newspaper <German: down into the garden>. Yes it is the dog. The dog wants the paper. The dog has the paper. Aah, the dog runs in front and takes the paper. Goes to the house. The dog reads the paper in front of the house. The old man smokes. Yes.

mhm. % här e de så att en man % sitter å somnar lite % framför huset / fram- framför ett hus. % de finns också en hund. (B:

MHM) % sen kommer en % pojke % som kastar tidningen in i garden. å hund tittar på. men man- mannen sova. (B: MHM) % sen % springar % s- springer hunden efter tidning. % och mannen märker ingenting. % hunden hämtar tidningen och går tillbaka till huset. kanske % tänker han ger tidningen till mannen. men % i alla fall i sist- / i den sista bilden så ser vi att % mannen har fortfarande ingen intresse. och hunden börja att+ läsa tidningen själv.

English gloss

Mmm. Here it is so that a man sits and falls asleep a little in front of a house. There is also a dog. (B:MHM) Then comes a boy who throws the newspaper into the garden. And dog watches. But the man sleep. (B:MHM) Then the dog runs after the paper. And the man notices nothing. The dog fetches the paper and goes back to the house. Perhaps he intends to give the paper to the man. But after all in the last picture we see that the man has still no interest. And the dog begins to read the paper himself.

References

Andersen, R. W. (1984) 'The one to one principle in interlanguage construction'. *Language Learning*, 34, 77–95.

Aronin, L. and D. Singleton (2008) 'Multilingualism as a new linguistic dispensation'. *International Journal of Multilingualism*, 5: 1–16.

Bannert, R. (1990) *På väg mot svenskt uttal*. Lund: Studentlitteratur.

Bardel, C. and Y. Falk (2007) 'The role of the second language in third language acquisition: The case of Germanic syntax'. *Second Language Research*, 24: 149–80.

Bardel, C. and C. Lindqvist (2006) 'The role of proficiency and psychotypology in lexical cross-linguistic influence. A study of a multilingual learner of Italian L3', in M. Chini, P. Desideri, M. E. Favilla and G. Pallotti (eds) *Atti del VI Congresso Internazionale dell'Associazione Italiana di Linguistica Applicata, Napoli, 9–10 febbraio 2006*. Perugia: Guerra Editore, pp. 123–45.

Bartning, I. (1992) 'L'activité interactionnelle dans une étude longitudinale de l'acquisition du français langue étrangère', in R. Bouchard, J. Billiez, J.-M. Colletta, V. de Nucheze and A. Millet (eds) *Acquisition et enseignement / apprentissage des langues. Actes du VIIIe Colloque International: Acquisition d'une langue étrangère: perspectives et recherches*. Grenoble: Lidilem, pp. 123–36.

Bialystok, E. (1983) 'Some factors in the selection and implementation of communication strategies', in C. Færch and G. Kasper (eds) *Strategies in Interlanguage Communication*. London and New York: Longman, pp. 100–18.

Biedermann, E. and A. Stedje (1975) 'Interferenzerscheinungen im Deutsch einiger finnischen Studenten beim Studium in Schweden', in H. Müssener and H. Rossipal (eds) *Impulse, Dank an Gustav Korlén zu seinem 60. Geburtstag*. Deutsches Institut, Universität Stockholm, pp. 231–58.

Bozier, C. (2005) *La sollicitation dans l'interaction exolingue en français*. PhD dissertation, Lund University, Dept of Romance Languages.

Burmeister, P. (1986) *Linguistische Untersuchung zum L2-Lexikonerwerb*. Magister dissertation, Englisches Seminar, Kiel University.

Bybee, J. L. (1998) 'The emergent lexicon'. *Publications of the Chicago Linguistic Society, 34.2: The Panels*, pp. 421–35.

Bybee, J. and P. Hopper (2001) 'Introduction to frequency and the emergence of linguistic structure', in J. Bybee and P. Hopper (eds) *Frequency and the Emergence of Linguistic Structure*. Amsterdam/Philadelphia: John Benjamins, pp. 1–24.

Cenoz, J. (2001) 'The effect of linguistic distance, L2 status and age on crosslinguistic influence in third language acquisition' in J. Cenoz, B. Hufeisen and U. Jessner (eds) *Cross-linguistic Influence in Third Language Acquisition: Psycholinguistic Perspectives*. Clevedon: Multilingual Matters, pp. 8–20.

Cenoz, J. (2003a) 'The additive effect of bilingualism on third language acquisition: A review'. *International Journal of Bilingualism*, 7: 71–87.

Cenoz, J. (2003b) 'The role of typology in the organization of the multilingual lexicon', in J. Cenoz, B. Hufeisen and U. Jessner (eds) *The Multilingual Lexicon*. Dordrecht, Boston and London: Kluwer, pp. 103–16.

Cenoz, J. (2005) 'Learning a third language: Cross-linguistic influence and its relationship to typology and age', in B. Hufeisen and R. J. Fouser (eds) *Introductory Readings in L3*, Tübingen: Stauffenburg Verlag, pp. 1–9.

Cenoz, J., B. Hufeisen and U. Jessner (eds) (2001) *Cross-linguistic Influence in Third Language Acquisition: Psycholinguistic Perspectives*. Clevedon: Multilingual Matters.

Cenoz, J., B. Hufeisen and U. Jessner (eds) (2003) *The Multilingual Lexicon*. Dordrecht, Boston and London: Kluwer, pp. 103–16.

Cenoz, J. and U. Jessner (eds) (2000) *English in Europe: The Acquisition of a Third Language*. Clevedon: Multilingual Matters.

Chandrasekhar, A. (1965). *A New Approach to Language Teaching*. Delhi: Linguistic Circle of Delhi.

Chandrasekhar, A. (1978) 'Base language'. *IRAL*, 16, 62–5.

Cook, V. J. (1991) 'The poverty of the stimulus argument and multicompetence'. *Second Language Research*, 7: 103–17.

Cook, V. J. (1992) 'Evidence for multicompetence'. *Language Learning*, 42: 557–91.

De Angelis, G. (2007) *Third or Additional Language Acquisition*. Clevedon: Multilingual Matters.

De Angelis, G. and L. Selinker (2001) 'Interlanguage transfer and competing linguistic systems in the multilingual mind', in J. Cenoz, B. Hufeisen and U. Jessner (eds) *Cross-linguistic Influence in Third Language Acquisition: Psycholinguistic Perspectives*. Clevedon: Multilingual Matters, pp. 42–58.

De Bot, K. (1992) 'A bilingual production model: Levelt's "Speaking" model adapted'. *Applied Linguistics*, 13, 1–24.

De Bot, K. (2004) 'The multilingual lexicon: Modelling selection and control'. *International Journal of Multilingualism*, 1, 17–32.

De Bot, K., T. S. Paribakht and M. B. Wesche (1997) 'Toward a lexical processing model for the study of second language acquisition: Evidence from ESL reading'. *Studies in Second Language Acquisition*, 19, 309–29.

De Groot, A. (1992) 'Bilingual lexical representation: A closer look at the conceptual representations', in R. Frost and L. Katz (eds) *Orthography, Phonology, Morphology, and Meaning*. Amsterdam: Elsevier.

De Pietro, J.-F., M. Matthey and B. Py (1989) 'Acquisition et contrat didactique: les séquences potentiellement acquisitionnelles de la conversation exolingue', in D. Weil and H. Fugier (eds) *Actes du troisième colloque régional de linguistique* Strasbourg: Université des sciences humaines et Université Louis Pasteur, pp. 99–124.

Dechert, H. W. (1984) 'Second language production: six hypotheses', in H. W. Dechert, D. Möhle and M. Raupach (eds) *Second Language Productions*. Tübingen: Gunter Narr Verlag.

Dechert, H. W. (1989) 'Competing plans in second language processing', in H. W. Dechert (ed.) *Current Trends in European Second Language Acquisition Research*. Clevedon and Philadelphia: Multilingual Matters.

Dewaele, J.-M. (1998) 'Lexical invention: French interlanguage as L2 versus L3'. *Applied Linguistics*, 19, 471–90.

Elert, C.-C. (1984) 'Forskning om tal, ljud och hörsel i en humanistisk omgivning', in L. Nord and P. af Trampe (eds) *Tal ljud hörsel 1*. Stockholm: Stockholms universitet, Institutionen för lingvistik, pp. 25–36.

Elert, C.-C. and Britta Hammarberg (1991) 'Regional voice quality variation in Sweden', in *Proceedings of the XIIth International Congress of Phonetic Sciences*, 4, 418–20. Aix-en-Provence: Université de Provence, Service des Publications.

Ellis, N. (2002) 'Frequency effects in language processing'. *Studies in Second Language Acquisition*, 18, 91–126.

Ellis, R. (1985) *Understanding Second Language Acquisition*. Oxford: Oxford University Press.

Ellis, R. (1994) *The Study of Second Language Acquisition*. Oxford: Oxford University Press.

Ericsson, K. A. and H. A. Simon (1984) *Verbal Reports as Data*. Cambridge, MA: The MIT Press.

Esling, J. H. (1978a) *Voice Quality in Edinburgh: A Sociolinguistic and Phonetic Study*. PhD dissertation, University of Edinburgh.

Esling, J. H. (1978b) 'The identification of features of voice quality in social groups'. *Journal of the International Phonetic Association*, 8, 18–23.

Færch, C. and G. Kasper (1983). 'Plans and strategies in foreign language communication', in C. Færch and G. Kasper (eds) *Strategies in Interlanguage Communication*. London and New York: Longman, pp. 20–60.

Færch, C. and G. Kasper (eds) (1987a) *Introspection in Second Language Research*. Clevedon: Multilingual Matters.

Færch, C. and G. Kasper (1987b) 'From product to process – introspective methods in second language research', in C. Færch and G. Kasper (eds) *Introspection in Second Language Research*. Clevedon: Multilingual Matters, pp. 5–23.

Fouser, R. J. (2001) 'Too close for comfort? Sociolinguistic transfer from Japanese into Korean as an L≥3', in J. Cenoz, B. Hufeisen and U. Jessner (eds) *Cross-linguistic Influence in Third Language Acquisition: Psycholinguistic Perspectives*. Clevedon: Multilingual Matters, pp. 149–69.

Garman, M. (1990) *Psycholinguistics*. Cambridge: Cambridge University Press.

Gick, B., I. Wilson, K. Koch and C. Cook (2004) 'Language-specific articulatory settings: Evidence from inter-utterance rest position'. *Phonetica*, 61, 220–33.

Giesbers, H. (1989) *Code-switching tussen Dialect en Standaardtaal*. Amsterdam: P. J. Meertens-Instituut.

Green, D. W. (1986) 'Control, activation and resource: A framework and a model for the control of speech in bilinguals'. *Brain and Language*, 27, 210–23.

Green, D. W. (1993) 'Towards a model of L2 comprehension and production', in R. Schreuder and B. Weltens (eds) *The Bilingual Lexicon*. Amsterdam and Philadelphia: John Benjamins, pp. 249–77.

Grosjean, F. (1982) *Life with Two Languages: An Introduction to Bilingualism*. Cambridge, MA: Harvard University Press.

Grosjean, F. (1995) 'A psycholinguistic approach to code-switching: the recognition of guest words by bilinguals', in L. Milroy and P. Muysken (eds) *One Speaker, Two Languages: Cross-disciplinary Perspectives on Code-switching*. Cambridge: Cambridge University Press, pp. 259–75.

Grosjean, F. (2001) 'The bilingual's language modes', in J. L. Nicol (ed.) *One Mind, Two Languages: Bilingual Language Processing*. Oxford: Blackwell, pp. 1–22.

Haastrup, K. (1985) 'Lexical inferencing – a study of procedures in reception'. *Scandinavian Working Papers on Bilingualism*, 5, 63–86.

Haastrup, K. (1987) 'Using thinking aloud and retrospection to uncover learners' lexical inferencing procedures', in C. Færch and G. Kasper (eds) *Introspection in Second Language Research*. Clevedon and Philadelphia: Multilingual Matters, pp. 197–212.

Haastrup, K. (1990) 'Developing learners' procedural knowledge in comprehension', in R. Phillipson, E. Kellerman, L. Selinker, M. Sharwood Smith and M. Swain (eds) *Foreign/ Second Language Pedagogy Research*. Clevedon and Philadelphia: Multilingual Matters, pp. 120–33.

Haastrup, K. (1991) *Lexical Inferencing Procedures or Talking about Words*. Tübingen: Gunter Narr Verlag.

Hakuta, K. (1986) *Mirror of Language: The Debate on Bilingualism*. New York: Basic Books.

Hammarberg, B. (1988) *Studien zur Phonologie des Zweitsprachenerwerbs*. Acta Universitatis Stockholmiensis, Stockholmer Germanistische Forschungen, 38. Stockholm: Almqvist & Wiksell International.

Hammarberg, B. (1998) 'The learner's word acquisition attempts in conversation', in D. Albrechtsen, B. Henriksen, I. M. Mees and E. Poulsen (eds) *Perspectives on Foreign and Second Language Pedagogy*. Odense: Odense University Press, pp. 177–90.

Hammarberg, B. (1999) *Manual of the ASU Corpus: A Longitudinal Text Corpus of Adult Learner Swedish with a Corresponding Part from Native Swedes*. Dept of Linguistics, Stockholm University.

Hammarberg, B. (2001) 'Roles of L1 and L2 in L3 production and acquisition', in J. Cenoz, B. Hufeisen and U. Jessner (eds) *Cross-linguistic Influence in Third Language Acquisition: Psycholinguistic Perspectives*. Clevedon: Multilingual Matters, pp. 21–41.

Hammarberg, B. (2006) 'Activation de L1 et L2 lors de la production orale en L3: Étude comparative de deux cas', *Acquisition et Interaction en Langue Étrangère (AILE)* 24, 45–74.

Hammarberg, Björn and Britta Hammarberg (1993) 'Articulatory re-setting in the acquisition of new languages', in E. Strangert, M. Heldner and P. Czigler (eds) (1993) *Studies Presented to Claes-Christian Elert on the Occasion of his Seventieth Birthday*. Reports from the Department of Phonetics, University of Umeå (PHONUM) 2, pp. 61–7.

Hammarberg, Björn and Britta Hammarberg (2005) 'Re-setting the basis of articulation in the acquisition of new languages: A third-language case study', in B. Hufeisen and R. Fouser (eds) *Introductory Readings in L3*. Tübingen: Stauffenburg, pp. 11–18.

Hammarberg, B. and S. Williams (1993) 'A study of third language acquisition', in B. Hammarberg (ed.) *Problem, Process, Product in Language Learning*. Stockholm University, Dept of Linguistics, pp. 60–70.

Heine, L. (2002) 'Der Einfluss vorher gelernter Sprachen auf das aktuelle Sprachenlernen. Ergebnisse einer empirischen Studie'. Paper presented at the Second International Conference on Third Language Acquisition and Trilingualism, Fryske Akademy, 13–15 September 2001, in M. Hooghiemstra (ed.) *Interactive CD-ROM, L3 Conference*. Ljouwert/Leeuwarden: Fryske Akademy.

Henriksson, Y. and H. Ringbom (1985) 'Linguistic and psycholinguistic approaches to multilingualism: A bibliography', in H. Ringbom (ed.) *Foreign Language Learning and Bilingualism*. Åbo: Åbo Akademi, pp. 191–201.

Herwig, A. (2001) 'Plurilingual lexical organisation: Evidence from lexical processing in L1–L2–L3–L4 translation', in J. Cenoz, B. Hufeisen and U. Jessner (eds) *Cross-linguistic Influence in Third Language Acquisition: Psycholinguistic Perspectives*. Clevedon: Multilingual Matters, pp. 115–37.

Herwig, A. (2004) *Aspects of Linguistic Organisation: Evidence from Lexical Processing in L1–L2 Translation*. Report from the Faculty of Education, Åbo Akademi University, 13. Vasa.

Honikman, B. (1964) 'Articulatory settings', in D. Abercrombie (ed.) *In Honour of Daniel Jones*. London: Longman, pp. 73–84.

Hufeisen, B. (1993) 'Fehleranalyse: English als L2 und Deutsch als L3'. *IRAL*, 31, 242–56.

Hufeisen, B. (1998) 'L3 – Stand der Forschung – Was bleibt zu tun?', in B. Hufeisen and B. Lindemann (eds) *Tertiärsprachen: Theorien, Modelle, Methoden*. Tübingen: Stauffenburg Verlag.

Hyltenstam, K. (1987) 'Markedness, language universals, language typology, and second language acquisition', in C. W. Pfaff (ed.) *First and Second Language Acquisition Processes*. New York: Newbury House, pp. 55–78.

Jenner, B. (2001) 'Articulatory setting: Genealogies of an idea'. *Historiographia Linguistica*, 28, 121–41.

Jessner, U. (2006) *Linguistic Awareness in Multilinguals*. Edinburgh: Edinburgh University Press.

Kellerman, E. (1977) 'Toward a characterization of the strategy of transfer in second language learning'. *Interlanguage Studies Bulletin*, 2, 58–145.

Kellerman, E. (1978) 'Giving learners a break: native language intuitions as a source of predictions about transferability'. *Working Papers on Bilingualism*, 15, 59–92.

Kellerman, E. (1983) 'Now you see it, now you don't', in S. Gass and L. Selinker (eds) *Language Transfer in Language Learning*. Rowley, MA: Newbury House, pp. 112–34.

Kelz, H. P. (1971) 'Articulatory basis and second language teaching'. *Phonetica*, 24, 193–211.

Kemmer, S. and M. Barlow (1999) 'Introduction: A usage-based conception of language', in M. Barlow and S. Kemmer (eds) *Usage-Based Models of Language*. Stanford: CSLI Publications, Center for the Study of Language and Information, pp. vii–xxvii.

Klein, E. C. (1995) 'Second versus third language acquisition: Is there a difference?'. *Language Learning*, 45/3, 419–65.

Korlén, G. and B. Malmberg (1993) *Tysk fonetik*. 6th edn. Malmö: Gleerups.

Kormos, J. (2006) *Speech Production and Second Language Acquisition*. New York and London: Lawrence Erlbaum Associates.

Langacker, R. W. (1988) 'A usage-based model', in B. Rudzka-Ostyn (ed.) *Topics in Cognitive Linguistics*. (Current Issues in Linguistic Theory, 50.) Amsterdam: John Benjamins.

Langacker, R. W. (1999) 'A dynamic usage-based model', in M. Barlow and S. Kemmer (eds) *Usage-Based Models of Language*. Stanford: CSLI Publications, Center for the Study of Language and Information, pp. 1–63.

Laver, J. (1978) 'The concept of articulatory settings: An historical survey'. *Historiographia Linguistica*, 5, pp. 1–14.

Laver, J. (1980) *The Phonetic Description of Voice Quality*. Cambridge: Cambridge University Press.

Laver, J. (1994) *Principles of Phonetics*. Cambridge: Cambridge University Press.

Laver, J. and P. Trudgill (1979) 'Phonetic and linguistic markers in speech', in K. L. Scherer and H. Giles (eds) *Social Markers in Speech*. Cambridge: Cambridge University Press, pp. 1–32.

Levelt, W. J. M. (1989) *Speaking: From Intention to Articulation*. Cambridge, MA: The MIT Press.

Levelt, W. J. M. (1993) 'The architecture of normal spoken language use', in G. Blanken, J. Dittmann, H. Grimm, J. C. Marschall and C.-W. Wallesch (eds) *Linguistic Disorders and Pathologies: An International Handbook*. Berlin and New York: De Gruyter, pp. 1–15.

Levelt, W. J. M. (1999) 'Producing spoken language: A blueprint of the speaker', in C. M. Brown and P. Hagoort (eds) *The Neurocognition of Language*. Oxford: Oxford University Press, pp. 83–122.

Levelt, W. J. M., A. Roelofs and A. S. Meyer, 'A theory of lexical access in speech production'. *Behavioral and Brain Sciences*, 22, 1–75.

Linell, P. (1998) *Approaching Dialogue: Talk, Interaction and Contents in Dialogical Perspectives*. Amsterdam and Philadelphia: John Benjamins.

Linell, P. and L. Gustavsson (1987) *Initiativ och respons. Om dialogens dynamik, dominans och koherens*. Studies in Communication, University of Linköping.

Mackey, W. F. (1967) *Bilingualism as a World Problem*. Montreal: Harvest House.

Mägiste, E. (1986) 'Selected issues in second and third language learning', in J. Vaid (ed.) *Language Processing in Bilinguals: Psycholinguistic and Neuropsychological Perspectives*. Hillsdale: Erlbaum, pp. 97–122.

McLaughlin, B. (1984) *Second-Language Acquisition in Childhood: Volume 1. Preschool Children*. 2nd edn. Hillsdale, NJ and London: Lawrence Erlbaum Associates.

Meisel, J. (1983) 'Transfer as a second language strategy'. *Language and Communication*, 3, 11–46.

Menn, L. and L. K. Obler (1990) *Agrammatic Aphasia*. Vol. 2. Amsterdam: John Benjamins.

Muysken, P. (1995) 'Code-switching and grammatical theory', in L. Milroy and P. Muysken (eds) *One Speaker, Two Languages: Cross-disciplinary Perspectives on Code-switching*. Cambridge: Cambridge University Press.

Myers-Scotton, C. (1993) *Duelling Languages. Grammatical Structure in Codeswitching*. Oxford: Clarendon Press.

Odlin, T. (1989) *Language Transfer*. Cambridge: Cambridge University Press.

Paradis, M. (1981) 'Neurolinguistic organization of a bilingual's two languages', in J. E. Copeland and P. W. Davis (eds) *The Seventh LACUS Forum*. Columbia, SC: Hornbeam Press, pp. 486–94.

Paradis, M. (1987) *The Assessment of Bilingual Aphasia*. Hillsdale: Erlbaum.

Paradis, M. (1989) 'Bilingual and polyglot aphasia', in F. Boller and J. Grafman (eds) *Handbook of Neuropsychology, Vol. 2*. Amsterdam: Elsevier Science Publishers, pp 117–40.

Pfaff, C. (1979) 'Constraints on language mixing: intrasentential code-switching and borrowing in Spanish/English'. *Language*, 55, 291–318.

Poulisse, N. (1997) 'Language production in bilinguals', in A. de Groot and J. Knoll (eds) *Tutorials in Bilingualism: Psycholinguistic Perspectives*. Hillsdale, NJ: Lawrence Erlbaum, pp. 201–24.

Poulisse, N. and T. Bongaerts (1994) 'First language use in second language production'. *Applied Linguistics*, 15, 36–57.

Poulisse, N., T. Bongaerts and E. Kellerman (1987) 'The use of retrospective verbal reports in the analysis of compensatory strategies', in C. Færch and G. Kasper (eds) *Strategies in Interlanguage Communication*. London and New York: Longman, pp. 213–29.

Py, B. (1990) 'Les stratégies d'acquisition en situation d'interaction', in D. Gaonac'h (ed.) *Acquisition et Utilisation d'une Langue Étrangère: l'approche cognitive*. Paris: Hachette, pp. 81–8.

Ridley, J. (1997) *Reflection and Strategies in Foreign Language Learning*. Frankfurt am Main: Peter Lang.

Ridley, J. and D. Singleton (1995a) 'Strategic L2 lexical innovation: Case study of a university-level *ab initio* learner of German'. *Second Language Research*, 11, pp. 137–48.

Ridley, J. and D. Singleton (1995b) 'Contrastivity and individual learner contrasts'. *Fremdsprachen Lehren und Lernen*, 24, 123–37.

Ringbom, H. (1982). 'The influence of other languages on the vocabulary of foreign language learners', in G. Nickel and D. Nehls (eds) *Error Analysis, Contrastive Linguistics and Second Language Learning. Papers from the 6th Congress of Applied Linguistics, Lund, 1981*. Heidelberg: Julius Groos Verlag, pp. 85–96.

Ringbom, H. (1983) 'Borrowing and lexical transfer'. *Applied Linguistics*, 4/3, 207–12.

Ringbom, H. (1985) 'The influence of Swedish on the English of Finnish learners', in H. Ringbom (ed.) *Foreign Language Learning and Bilingualism*. Publications of the Research Institute of the Åbo Akademi Foundation 105. Åbo: Åbo Akademi, pp. 39–71.

Ringbom, H. (1987) *The Role of the First Language in Foreign Language Learning*. Clevedon: Multilingual Matters.

Ringbom, H. (2007) *Cross-linguistic Similarity in Foreign Language Learning*. Clevedon: Multilingual Matters.

Schegloff, E. A., G. Jefferson and H. Sacks (1977) 'The preference for self-correction in the organisation of self-repair in conversation'. *Language*, 53, 361–82.

Selinker, L. (1972) 'Interlanguage'. *IRAL*, 10, 209–31.

Sharwood Smith, M. (1994) *Second Language Learning*. London and New York: Longman.

Singleton, D. (1999) *Exploring the Second Language Mental Lexicon*. Cambridge: Cambridge University Press.

Singleton, D. and M. Ó Laoire (2006) '"Psychotypologie" et "facteur L2" dans l'influence translexicale: une analyse de l'influence de l'anglais et de l'irlandais sur le français de l'apprenant L3.' *Acquisition et Interaction en Langue Étrangère (AILE)* 24, 101–17.

Stedje, A. (1977) 'Tredjespråksinterferens i fritt tal – en jämförande studie', in R. Palmberg and H. Ringbom (eds) *Papers from the Conference on Contrastive Linguistics and Error Analysis. Stockhom and Åbo, 7–8 February, 1977*. Åbo: Åbo Akademi, pp. 141–58.

Tarone, E. (1982) 'Systematicity and attention in interlanguage'. *Language Learning*, 32, 69–82.

Tarone, E. (1985) 'Variability in interlanguage use: A study of style-shifting in morphology and syntax'. *Language Learning*, 35, 373–404.

Tarone, E., A. D. Cohen and G. Dumas (1983) 'A closer look at some interlanguage terminology: A framework for communication strategies', in C. Færch and G. Kasper (eds) *Strategies in Interlanguage Communication*. London and New York: Longman, pp. 4–14.

Ternström, S. (1990) *Soundswell – Signal Workstation Software. Manual Version 3.0*. Stockholm: Soundswell Music Acoustics HB.

Thomas, M. (1990) 'Acquisition of the Japanese reflexive *zibu* by unilingual and multilingual learners', in H. Burmeister and P. Rounds (eds) *Variability in Second Language Acquisition: Proceedings of the Tenth Meeting of the Second Language Research Forum*. Eugene: University of Oregon.

Trudgill, P. (1974) *The Social Differentiation of English in Norwich*. Cambridge: Cambridge University Press.

Tucker, G. R. (1998) 'A global perspective on multilingualism and multilingual education', in J. Cenoz and F. Genesee (eds) *Beyond Bilingualism: Multilingualism and Multilingual Education*. Clevedon: Multilingual Matters, pp. 3–15.

Vasseur, M.-T. (1990) 'Interaction et acquisition d'une langue étrangère en milieu social', in D. Gaonac'h (ed.) *Acquisition et Utilisation d'une Langue Étrangère: l'approche cognitive*. Paris: Hachette, pp. 89–100.

Vildomec, V. (1963) *Multilingualism*. Leyden: A. W. Sythoff.

Vogel, T. (1992) '"Englisch und Deutsch gibt es immer Krieg". Sprachverarbeitungsprozesse beim Erwerb des Deutschen als Drittsprache'. *Zielsprache Deutsch*, 23, 95–9. English version (2005) '"German and English, they're always fighting": Language assimilation processes in the acquisition of German as a third language', in B. Hufeisen and R. Fouser (eds) *Introductory Readings in L3*. Tübingen: Stauffenburg, pp. 111–16.

Wängler, H. H. (1974) *Grundriss einer Phonetik des Deutschen*. 3rd edn. Marburg: Elwert.

Weinreich, U. (1953) *Languages in Contact. Findings and Problems*. 3rd printing, 1964. The Hague: Mouton.

Williams, S. and B. Hammarberg (1994) 'An L3 learner's lexicon expansion attempts during interaction'. Paper presented at EUROSLA, Aix-en-Provence, 1994.

Williams, S. and B. Hammarberg (1998) 'Language switches in L3 production: Implications for a polyglot speaking model'. *Applied Linguistics*, 19, 295–333.

Wilson, I. L. (2006) *Articulatory Settings of French and English Monolingual and Bilingual Speakers*. PhD dissertation, University of British Columbia. Accessed 8 February 2008 from http://www.u-aizu.ac.jp/~wilson/Wilson2006PhD.pdf.

Wode, H., A. Rohde, F. Gassen, B. Weiss, M. Jekat and P. Jung (1992) 'L1, L2, L3: continuity vs discontinuity in lexical acquisition', in P. J. L. Arnaud and H. Béjoint (eds) *Vocabulary and Applied Linguistics*. London: Macmillan, pp. 52–61.

Index

activation, 8–9, 12, 32–4, 63, 101–2, 105, 111, 117–26, 127–8, 130, 133–4, 144, 147–50, 152n

active language, 8–9, 12, 32–3, 39, 102, 121, 133, 150

Andersen, 66

Aronin, 3

articulatory settings, 13, 74–5, 125, 136, 150

Artikulationsbasis *see* articulatory settings

avoidance strategy, 29

background language, 1, 6, 8, 10, 12–14, 28, 39, 65, 96, 101–5, 111–24, 127–33, 138–9, 143–7

Bannert, 136

Bardel, 83, 123–4

Barlow, 9

Bartning, 87, 97, 115

basis of articulation *see* articulatory settings

Biedermann, 18

bilingual mode *see* language mode

Bongaerts, 9, 21, 29–35, 38, 42, 64–5, 133–4

Bozier, 87, 115

Burmeister, 34

Bybee, 9

Cenoz, 2, 83, 101, 123

Chandrasekhar, 36, 63, 67, 123

code-switching *see* language switch

comprehension, 7–8, 86, 129; *see also* reception of speech

content word, 30–1, 34–5, 37, 47–9, 56, 64–6, 88, 108–13, 120, 124, 134–5, 150

Cook, V. J., 3, 9, 68

creative lexical construction *see* creative word construction

creative word construction, 15, 129, 137, 147, 151; *see also* word construction

crosslinguistic influence, 1, 4, 8, 10, 18, 28, 32, 36, 53, 63, 79, 83, 112, 127–30, 137, 144–5, 147, 150

crosslinguistic similarity, 14–15, 83, 127–36, 141, 145, 151; *see also* typological similarity, perceived crosslinguistic similarity, language distance

De Angelis, 5, 83, 128

De Bot, 3, 8–9, 31–3, 39, 63, 65, 67–8, 86, 118–20, 133, 145, 152n

De Groot, 33

De Pietro, 87, 89, 115

Dechert, 29